The Hollywood Bowl Cookbook

Picnics Under the Stars

The Hollywood Bowl Cookbook: Picnics Under the Stars

Published by the Los Angeles Philharmonic Affiliates of the
    Los Angeles Philharmonic Association
Copyright © 2002 by the Los Angeles Philharmonic Affiliates
    of the Los Angeles Philharmonic Association
135 North Grand Avenue
Los Angeles, California 90012
(213) 972-7300

This cookbook is a collection of favorite recipes, which are not necessarily original recipes.

ISBN: 0-9716124-0-4
Library of Congress Catalog Number: 2002101135

Edited, designed, and manufactured by
Favorite Recipes® Press, an imprint of

FRP

2451 Atrium Way
Nashville, Tennessee 37214
1-800-358-0560

Art Director: Steve Newman
Managing Editor: Mary Cummings
Project Manager: Judy Jackson
Project Editor: Debbie Van Mol

Manufactured in the United States of America
First Printing: 2002   7,500 copies

Cover photograph by Otto Rothschild, October 15, 1945
Courtesy of the Music Center Archives, Otto Rothschild Collection
Reproduction without permission prohibited
Hand-tinted by Christina Angarola
Program covers courtesy of the Hollywood Bowl Museum

TABLE OF CONTENTS

INTRODUCTION

The next time you visit the Hollywood Bowl, take a moment to look around you. Everywhere, you see people picnicking with friends while they wait for the concert to start. Whether they are anticipating a Los Angeles Philharmonic concert or a Hollywood Bowl Orchestra program, a jazz or World Festival performance, or another event hosted by the Bowl, they know that good food and good friends at the Bowl combine to create an ideal setting for great music. In celebration of the bucolic Hollywood Bowl and its time-honored tradition of bringing together music, friends, and picnics, the Philharmonic Affiliates have gathered the recipes that appear in this Cookbook.

The Affiliates support the Philharmonic in many ways. They promote ticket sales, they fundraise, they support the Philharmonic's educational activities, and they do so much more. May the success of the Hollywood Bowl Cookbook encourage the Philharmonic Affiliates to continue their good work on behalf of our orchestra and our special summer home, the Hollywood Bowl.

Deborah Borda
Executive Vice President and Managing Director
Los Angeles Philharmonic Association

PICNICS UNDER THE STARS

By the late afternoon of most summer nights, just when the sky is cooling from hot orange into streaky pink and blue, throngs of people filter slowly into the Hollywood Bowl. Some have carried elaborate picnic baskets up the hill from city buses; others have hauled coolers and shopping bags from the parking lots jammed with cars; yet more have arrived in limousines and taxis with gourmet carryout and chilled bottles of Champagne. All of these comestible goods will be enjoyed with indulgent pleasure at the Bowl's many picnic sites.

Some music lovers feast at picnic tables in grassy areas amid overhanging ivy, eucalyptus, lemon, and California pepper trees; some on the amphitheater benches; some in private boxes (the ultimate luxury); and some even on blankets spread along the walkways leading into the Bowl, everyone anticipating and relishing the same exciting, charged atmosphere of a unique outdoor dining experience with musical feasting to follow.

And what food! From picnic baskets come offerings of leafy salads and pasta salads, submarine sandwiches and chocolate chip cookies, sushi and sashimi, poached salmon and roasted chicken, fruit tarts and quiches, baguettes and cheeses, desserts and coffees, wines and beers. From humble food to catered spreads, variety and ingenuity abound. In a setting enhanced by fresh flowers, candles, silver, and china, or just festive paper goods and plastics, everyone is enjoying the most popular summer evening pastime in Los Angeles.

This is the experience known as an evening at the Hollywood Bowl. This is the experience captured in *The Hollywood Bowl Cookbook: Picnics Under the Stars*.

FOREWORD

One of Los Angeles' ultimate experiences is al fresco dining underneath the stars at the Hollywood Bowl. The exquisite fusion of live music, fine food, and a balmy summer breeze is unmatched— you are immediately transported from the mundane to the sublime.

Since its inception in 1922, the Hollywood Bowl has captivated millions by presenting the finest in musical talent. Today, The Patina Group is proud to be selected as the official caterer and food service provider for the Hollywood Bowl. We have worked hard to create a harmonious balance between our cuisine and the musical experience, which is something not to be missed.

Throughout *The Hollywood Bowl Cookbook: Picnics Under the Stars*, you'll find culinary creations that incorporate the old with the new—classic tastes with modern twists to delight your senses, just like a fine Hollywood Bowl performance. While the Bowl's musical season runs only through the summer months, you can recreate fine cuisine at any time of the year with this magnificent cookbook.

Bon appétit,

Joachim Splichal

Joachim Splichal
Chef and founder of The Patina Group

LOS ANGELES PHILHARMONIC AFFILIATES

With approximately 1,000 volunteers in thirteen independent committees throughout Southern California, the Los Angeles Philharmonic Affiliates constitute one of the largest and most active major symphony orchestra support groups in the country. The Affiliates' purpose is to support the Los Angeles Philharmonic in all its activities through the promotion of volunteerism, fund-raising, ticket sales, and youth music education programs.

We believe that "Music Matters" in the lives of young people, and we work tirelessly to promote that concept through participation in the Symphonies for Schools program and the Toyota Symphonies for Youth Concerts. The Affiliates also manage the Music Mobile program, providing a hands-on classroom experience for thousands of students in the Los Angeles Basin. We contribute to a Student/Braille Ticket Fund, underwrite the Bronislaw Kaper Awards, an instrumental competition, and organize a Student Invitational Rehearsal Program. These education and community programs touch the lives of at least 100,000 young people each year.

Proceeds realized from the sale of *The Hollywood Bowl Cookbook: Picnics Under the Stars* will be used for the music education projects we sponsor in the community and for the support of our inspiring Los Angeles Philharmonic Orchestra and Hollywood Bowl Orchestra. To them we dedicate our book.

ACKNOWLEDGMENTS

COOKBOOK COMMITTEE

Mary Anne Chappelear
Jan Corey
Marilyn Dale
Judith Epley
Joy McCarthy
Olive McDuffee
Judy Munro

Lois Petrovich
Sarah Reinhart
Erika Riley
Doris Segall
Carol Sandmeier
Denise Smith
Joan Stubbs

THE LOS ANGELES PHILHARMONIC STAFF
who were always there to help

Glenn Baker
Deborah Borda
Vanessa Butler
David Chambers
Gretchen Citrin
Catherine Scanlon Cowles
Joan Cumming
Vicki Friedman
Paul Gibson

Melanie Gravdal
Beth Taylor Hart
Emily Laskin
Carol Merrill-Mirsky, Ph.D.
Patricia Mitchell
Jan Moya
Elizabeth R. Shafer
Bill Wilson

ADDITIONAL SUPPORT WAS RECEIVED FROM

Julio Gonzales, Archivist, Los Angeles Music Center
Joan Nielsen, Consultant

The Cookbook Committee wishes to thank Kendall-Jackson Wines
for their great interest in wine and food and their help in preparing this cookbook.

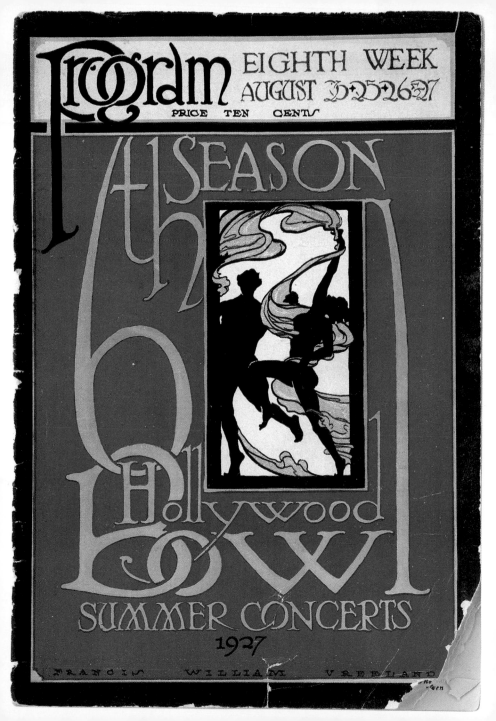

APPETIZERS

ARTICHOKE SQUARES

3 (6-ounce) jars marinated artichoke hearts

1 cup chopped onion

2 garlic cloves, crushed or finely chopped

8 eggs

1 pound sharp Cheddar cheese, shredded

1/2 cup seasoned bread crumbs

1/4 cup minced fresh parsley

1/2 teaspoon salt

1/4 teaspoon oregano

1/4 teaspoon pepper

1/4 teaspoon Tabasco sauce

Sprigs of watercress or parsley

Drain the oil from 1 jar of the artichokes into a 12-inch skillet, reserving the artichokes. Heat the oil over medium heat. Sauté the onion and garlic in the hot oil for 5 minutes. Drain the remaining 2 jars of artichokes, discarding the oil. Chop finely the artichokes from all 3 jars.

Whisk the eggs in a bowl until foamy. Stir in the cheese, bread crumbs, 1/4 cup parsley, salt, oregano, pepper and Tabasco sauce. Add the artichokes and mix well. Stir in the sautéed onion mixture.

Spoon the artichoke mixture into 2 greased 9x9-inch baking pans. Bake at 325 degrees for 30 minutes. Cut each pan into 16 squares. Serve hot or at room temperature garnished with sprigs of watercress or parsley. You may substitute crumbled feta cheese for the Cheddar cheese.

Makes 32 squares

EMPANADAS

These hearty "pockets" are eaten throughout Latin America from Mexico to Argentina, and make an international addition to any picnic.

Pastry
1 3/4 cups flour
1/2 teaspoon salt
1/2 cup (1 stick) unsalted butter, chilled, cut into quarters
1/4 cup ice water
3 tablespoons canola oil

Filling and Assembly
1/2 cup shredded queso blanco or Monterey Jack cheese
1/4 cup sliced green olives
1/4 cup chopped green onions
Milk

For the pastry, combine the flour and salt in a food processor bowl fitted with a metal blade. Add the butter quarters 1 at a time, processing constantly until of the consistency of a coarse meal.

Pour the flour mixture into a medium bowl. Mix the ice water and canola oil in a bowl. Add the ice water mixture to the flour mixture and stir with a fork until the mixture adheres. Separate the dough into 6 equal portions. Roll or pat each portion into a 1/4-inch-thick circle.

For the filling, sprinkle the cheese, olives and green onions equally over half of each circle. Fold over to enclose the filling, crimping the edges with a fork. Brush the tops lightly with milk. Arrange the empanadas on a baking sheet. Bake at 400 degrees for 15 to 20 minutes or until golden brown. Serve hot or cold.

Makes 6 empanadas

Where is the Hollywood Bowl? The Bowl is located in the heart of Los Angeles, one-half mile north of Hollywood Boulevard. It is directly off the historic Cahuenga Pass, the site of El Camino Real, the original route connecting California's missions. Southern California's freeways now link the Bowl to outlying communities in all directions.

RATATOUILLE ON TOASTS

2 tablespoons olive oil
1 medium eggplant, chopped
1 onion, chopped
1 red bell pepper, chopped
1 garlic clove, minced
2 large tomatoes, peeled, chopped
1/4 cup sliced black or Spanish olives
1 tablespoon drained capers
1 teaspoon rosemary
1 teaspoon thyme
3 tablespoons red wine vinegar
2 tablespoons balsamic vinegar
1 teaspoon sugar
1 baguette sourdough bread, thinly sliced, heated

Heat the olive oil in a nonreactive skillet over medium heat. Sauté the eggplant, onion, bell pepper and garlic in the hot oil until light brown. Stir in the tomatoes.

Cook just until blended, stirring frequently. Stir in the olives, capers, rosemary and thyme. Simmer for 20 minutes, stirring occasionally. Add the wine vinegar, balsamic vinegar and sugar and mix well.

Simmer for 15 minutes longer, stirring occasionally. Let stand until cool. Chill, covered, for 8 to 10 hours or for up to 1 week. Serve at room temperature with warm baguette slices.

Serves 8 to 10

SPICY ITALIAN CHICKEN FINGERS

These unusual bites are "finger-lickin' good" and may be served hot right out of the oven, or chilled and then transported to your Hollywood Bowl picnic.

1 pound boneless skinless chicken breasts, cut into 1-inch strips
1/4 cup spicy vegetable juice cocktail
2 tablespoons olive oil
1/4 teaspoon oregano
1/8 teaspoon red pepper flakes
6 tablespoons Italian bread crumbs
1/4 cup grated Romano cheese

Combine the chicken, vegetable juice cocktail, olive oil, oregano and red pepper flakes in a sealable plastic bag and seal tightly. Shake to coat. Marinate in the refrigerator for 1 hour or longer, turning occasionally.

Combine the bread crumbs and cheese in a bowl and mix well. Add the crumb mixture to the chicken and shake to coat. Arrange the chicken in a single layer on a baking sheet sprayed with nonstick cooking spray. Bake at 475 degrees for 8 minutes.

Serves 4

1900 *Picnics actually predated music at the Hollywood Bowl. Hollywood residents often carried picnic baskets into what was then called Daisy Dell.*

CHICKEN FRITTERS

This staple from India, given to us by Zubin Mehta's mother, does not last long on the buffet table and is a hearty addition to any picnic.

4 ounces chick-pea (garbanzo) flour

2 ounces white flour

1 teaspoon salt

1/4 teaspoon chili powder, red pepper or cayenne pepper, or to taste

1/4 teaspoon baking powder

2 eggs, beaten

2 teaspoons lemon juice

1/2 cup (about) water

3 pounds chicken breasts, boned, skinned, cut into 1-inch strips

Vegetable oil for deep-frying

Combine the chick-pea flour, white flour, salt, chili powder and baking powder in a bowl and mix well. Stir in the eggs and lemon juice. Add just enough water until the batter is thick enough to coat the chicken and mix well. Add the chicken and stir until coated.

Pour the oil into a wok or heavy skillet to a depth of 2 inches. Heat the oil to 375 degrees. Drop the chicken into the hot oil using tongs. Fry for 5 minutes or until the chicken is golden brown; drain. Serve immediately. Chick-pea flour is available in Indian markets.

Serves 6

COCKTAIL SHRIMP WITH MANGO CHUTNEY

Mangoes are available in the produce department or in jars in the canned goods section of most supermarkets.

2 medium shallots, minced
1 tablespoon grated peeled fresh gingerroot
1 tablespoon vegetable oil
2 mangoes, peeled, cut into 1/4-inch pieces
1/3 cup sugar
1 1/2 teaspoons chile flakes
1/3 cup Champagne vinegar
1/3 cup minced fresh mint leaves
1/2 teaspoon salt
Fresh mint leaves
1 pound cooked shrimp, peeled, deveined

Sauté the shallots and gingerroot in the oil in a skillet. Stir in the mangoes, sugar and chile flakes. Cook until the mangoes are tender, stirring occasionally. Stir in the vinegar.

Cook until thickened, stirring frequently. Add the minced mint and salt and mix well. Remove from heat. Let stand until cool. Spoon the chutney into a serving bowl. Garnish with mint leaves. Serve with the shrimp.

Serves 6 to 8

1919   *On May 30, Charles Toberman, known as the "father of Hollywood," working with a newly formed Theatre Arts Alliance, secured an option from owner Myra Hershey to purchase Daisy Dell for $20,000. On June 2, he finalized an option with James Lacey, of Lacey Carpet Cleaning Company, for $7,000 for the land that would become the seating area of the Hollywood Bowl. Then he negotiated an option with mail carrier Herbert Teele, who owned property near the entrance to the Bowl at Cahuenga Pass, for the princely sum of $22,000.*

GINGER-SPIKED SHRIMP

1 cup sake
1 cup rice vinegar
1/4 cup soy sauce
2 tablespoons brown sugar
2 tablespoons chopped pickled ginger
12 large shrimp (16 to 20 count), peeled, deveined
Wasabi Crème Fraîche (below)

Combine the sake, vinegar, soy sauce, brown sugar and ginger in a saucepan and mix well. Cook until reduced by half, stirring occasionally. Stir in the shrimp. Sauté until the shrimp turn pink and are firm. Chill, covered, in the refrigerator immediately. Serve with Wasabi Crème Fraîche.

Serves 2 to 3

WASABI CREME FRAICHE

1 cup packed fresh spinach leaves
1 cup crème fraîche or sour cream
1/3 cup fresh cilantro
2 tablespoons rice vinegar
1 tablespoon prepared wasabi
Salt and pepper to taste

Combine the spinach leaves, crème fraîche, cilantro, vinegar, wasabi, salt and pepper in a blender container. Process until puréed.

Makes 1 1/2 cups

CHICKEN PATE

For an exotic change of taste, substitute duck breasts for the chicken breasts.

1 medium carrot, chopped

1 1/2 pounds boneless skinless
   chicken breasts, cut into chunks

3/4 cup heavy cream

1/2 cup dry white wine

1/2 cup coarsely chopped onion

4 egg whites

1/2 teaspoon salt

1 cup firmly packed fresh basil leaves

1 egg yolk

Blueberry Ketchup (page 19)

Whole grain or rye crackers

Combine the carrot with enough water to cover in a saucepan. Simmer until tender; drain. Process the chicken in a food processor fitted with a metal blade until finely chopped. Add the heavy cream, wine, onion, egg whites and salt. Process until smooth and creamy. Spoon 2 cups of the chicken mixture into a generously greased 4x8-inch loaf pan.

Divide the remaining chicken mixture into 2 equal portions. Combine 1 portion with the basil in a food processor bowl. Process until the basil is finely chopped and evenly combined. Spread the basil mixture over the prepared layer. Process the remaining chicken portion, carrot and egg yolk in a food processor until smooth. Spread evenly over the basil layer.

Bake at 350 degrees for 50 to 60 minutes or until the top is firm to the touch. Cool in pan on a wire rack until room temperature. Chill, covered, for 8 to 10 hours. Invert the pâté onto a platter and slice. Spread the Blueberry Ketchup on whole grain or rye crackers and top with a slice of the pâté. Arrange the crackers on a serving platter.

Serves 8 to 10

1920   *Several recognized artists tested the incredible acoustics of the new Hollywood Bowl, using a discarded door from the Lacey Carpet Cleaning Company as an impromptu stage. Among them was the great Madame Schumann-Heink, who sang Brahms' "Lullaby."*

BLUEBERRY KETCHUP

8 ounces fresh or frozen blueberries

1/2 cup sugar

2 tablespoons raspberry vinegar

1/2 teaspoon cinnamon

1/4 teaspoon freshly ground pepper

1/8 teaspoon allspice

1/8 teaspoon nutmeg

1/8 teaspoon ground cloves

Combine the blueberries, sugar, vinegar, cinnamon, pepper, allspice, nutmeg and cloves in a saucepan and mix well. Bring to a boil; reduce the heat.

Simmer for 20 minutes, stirring occasionally. Let stand until cool. Force the sauce through a food mill or serve as is. Serve at room temperature. You may microwave the blueberry mixture in a microwave-safe dish on High for 10 minutes.

Serves 8 to 10

OYSTER PATE

A real treat for oyster lovers and those who do not even think they like oysters.

1 (8-ounce) can whole oysters,
   drained, chopped

3 ounces cream cheese, softened

2 tablespoons minced green onions

1 tablespoon prepared horseradish

Lemon juice to taste

Chopped fresh parsley

Chopped walnuts (optional)

Combine the oysters, cream cheese, green onions, horseradish and lemon juice in a blender container. Process until smooth. Spoon the pâté into a serving bowl. Chill, covered, for 8 to 10 hours; the pâté will be semisoft. Sprinkle with the parsley and walnuts. Serve with assorted party crackers.

For a smoky oyster flavor, add 1/2 can of chopped drained smoked oysters, an additional 3 ounces softened cream cheese and additional lemon juice.

Serves 4 to 6

CORNED BEEF CHEESE BALL

8 ounces cream cheese, softened

2 cups shredded Cheddar cheese

1 (12-ounce) can corned beef, drained, shredded

3/4 cup sweet pickle relish

3 tablespoons fresh lemon juice

2 teaspoons prepared horseradish

1 1/2 teaspoons prepared mustard

1/2 teaspoon Worcestershire sauce

1/2 teaspoon grated lemon zest

1 cup minced fresh parsley

Beat the cream cheese and Cheddar cheese in a mixing bowl until blended. Stir in the corned beef, pickle relish, lemon juice, horseradish, prepared mustard, Worcestershire sauce and lemon zest.

Shape the cream cheese mixture into a ball and wrap tightly in foil. Chill for 30 minutes. Roll in the parsley. Serve with assorted party crackers and/or apple wedges.

Serves 12 to 15

EGGPLANT APPETIZER

3 long Japanese eggplant

2 medium tomatoes, chopped, or 4 Roma tomatoes, chopped

3 scallions, thinly sliced

1/4 cup chopped fresh parsley

1/4 cup olive oil, or to taste

2 tablespoons red wine vinegar

1 teaspoon salt

1/8 teaspoon sugar

Ground pepper to taste

Arrange the eggplant on a baking sheet. Bake at 350 degrees for 35 minutes or until tender. Peel and coarsely chop. Chill, covered, in a bowl.

Combine the chilled eggplant, tomatoes, scallions and parsley in a bowl and mix gently. Whisk the olive oil, vinegar, salt, sugar and pepper in a bowl. Pour over the eggplant mixture and toss to coat. Chill, covered, for several hours. Serve with assorted party crackers or breads.

You may substitute 1 medium regular eggplant for the Japanese eggplant. Peel and coarsely chop the eggplant. Combine with enough water to cover in a saucepan. Cook until tender, or microwave in a microwave-safe dish for about 3 minutes.

Serves 6 to 8

FABULOUS CHEESE MOUSSE

1 tablespoon unflavored gelatin
1/4 cup cold water
1 (1 1/3-ounce) package Camembert
   cheese
3 (1 1/4-ounce) packages Roquefort
   cheese
1 egg yolk, lightly beaten

1 tablespoon sherry
1 teaspoon Worcestershire sauce
1 egg white, stiffly beaten
1/2 cup chilled whipping cream,
   stiffly beaten
Sliced olives

Sprinkle the gelatin over the cold water in a heatproof bowl. Let stand for 5 minutes or until softened. Place the bowl over hot water to completely dissolve the gelatin and mix well. Force the Camembert cheese and Roquefort cheese through a sieve.

Combine the Camembert cheese, Roquefort cheese, egg yolk, sherry and Worcestershire sauce in a mixing bowl. Beat until blended. Stir in the gelatin mixture. Fold the egg white and whipped cream into the cheese mixture. Spoon into a 1-pint mold.

Chill, covered, for several hours or until firm. Invert onto a chilled serving platter. Garnish with sliced olives. Serve with assorted party crackers. To avoid raw eggs that may carry salmonella, we suggest using an equivalent amount of pasteurized egg substitute.

Serves 4 to 6

1921 *The first Easter service was directed and presented from a small wooden platform. About 800 people sat on wooden benches, and the rest spread blankets on the ground and worshiped picnic-style. On the Saturday before Easter, a children's choir met to plant fir trees on the hillside.*

21

CALIFORNIA-STYLE HUMMUS

This intriguing hors d'oeuvre can be stored in the refrigerator for up to three days. Tahini may be purchased in Middle Eastern markets and is now available in many supermarkets.

1 (15-ounce) can garbanzo beans
3 or 4 green onions
1/4 cup lemon juice
1/4 cup tahini (sesame paste), stirred
2 garlic cloves, crushed

1 teaspoon cumin
1/4 teaspoon freshly ground black
    pepper
1/8 teaspoon cayenne pepper
Chopped fresh parsley

Drain the beans, reserving 1/4 cup of the liquid. Rinse and drain the beans. Combine the beans, green onions and 2 tablespoons of the reserved liquid in a blender container. Process until puréed. Add the remaining 2 tablespoons reserved liquid, lemon juice, tahini, garlic, cumin, black pepper and cayenne pepper.

    Process until smooth. Taste and adjust the seasonings. Chill, covered, in the refrigerator for 3 hours or longer. Spoon the hummus into a shallow bowl or spread on a plate. Sprinkle with parsley. Serve with crudités and/or pita bread wedges.

Makes 1 1/2 cups

1921 *"It looks just like a big bowl!" said Hugo Kirchhofer in the autumn when he conducted a Community Sing in the new venue. The name stuck.*

SPINACH DIP IN RED CABBAGE BOWL

Here is an eye-catching recipe that also allows you to enjoy the five daily servings of vegetables recommended for healthy living. Use your imagination with the crudités.

2 cups finely chopped fresh spinach, or
    1 (10-ounce) package frozen chopped spinach
1 cup plain yogurt
1/2 cup mayonnaise
1/2 cup minced fresh cilantro
1/2 cup minced green onions with tops
1/2 cup minced artichoke bottoms
1 teaspoon dillweed
1/4 teaspoon seasoned salt
Freshly ground pepper to taste
1 large head red cabbage

Steam the fresh spinach until tender; drain. If using frozen spinach cook using package directions. Let stand until cool.

Combine the spinach, yogurt, mayonnaise, cilantro, green onions, artichokes, dillweed, seasoned salt and pepper in a bowl and mix well. Chill, covered, until serving time.

Scoop out the center of the cabbage, leaving a shell. Spoon the spinach dip into the shell just before serving. Serve with assorted crudités such as carrots, celery, red and green bell peppers, jicama, sugar peas and cauliflower.

Serves 6 to 8

UNIQUE VEGGIE DIP

The combination of these ingredients makes fresh vegetables really appealing to dip lovers.

1 cup cottage cheese or sour cream
1 cup mayonnaise
1 tablespoon finely chopped green onions
$1^1/2$ teaspoons chopped fresh parsley
$1^1/2$ teaspoons dillweed
$^1/4$ teaspoon curry powder
$^1/8$ teaspoon salt

Combine the cottage cheese, mayonnaise, green onions, parsley, dillweed, curry powder and salt in a bowl and mix well. Chill, covered, until serving time. Serve with fresh vegetables.

Serves 6 to 8

QUICK TAPENADE DIP

1 cup mayonnaise
1 (2-ounce) can anchovies, drained, chopped
1 (3-ounce) jar capers, drained
1 tablespoon lemon juice
1 garlic clove, minced
1 teaspoon Dijon mustard

Combine the mayonnaise, anchovies, capers, lemon juice, garlic and Dijon mustard in a blender container. Process until smooth. Chill, covered, until serving time. Serve with fresh vegetables.

Serves 6 to 8

ITZHAK PERLMAN'S VERY FATTENING CHOPPED CHICKEN LIVERS

Mr. Perlman says, "Make sure you have plenty of antacids...but it's worth it."

1 pound chicken fat, rendered

1 pound chicken livers

1 medium onion, finely chopped

3 hard-cooked eggs

Salt to taste

Pour the rendered fat into a large cast-iron skillet. Bring to a boil over high heat. Stir in the chicken livers. Cook for 6 minutes, stirring occasionally. Add the onion and mix well.

   Cook until the onion is light brown and the livers are cooked through, stirring occasionally. Partially drain the livers in a very fine metal colander. Chop the livers and eggs together in a bowl. Season with salt. Serve with matzoh or rye bread. For a sharper flavor, add raw chopped onions (that's the way my mother used to make it).

Wine Selection: Kendall-Jackson Vintner's Reserve Riesling

Serves 12 to 15

1922   *Artie Mason Carter, who earned the informal title of "Mother of the Hollywood Bowl," was able to bring together her Hollywood Community Sing and the recently formed Los Angeles Philharmonic in the Bowl for an Easter Sunrise Service before a reported audience of 5,000 people. The success of the Easter service inspired Mrs. Carter to suggest a series of summer concerts, and there was a major effort to get the Bowl into shape physically, financially, and artistically, even to planting hundreds of red geraniums to cover some of the bare, dusty areas.*

SALMON LOG

1 (15-ounce) can red salmon, drained
8 ounces cream cheese, softened
1 tablespoon lemon juice
2 teaspoons grated onion

^{1}/4 teaspoon salt
^{1}/4 teaspoon liquid smoke
^{3}/4 cup chopped pecans
3 tablespoons minced fresh parsley

Discard the skin and bones from the salmon. Flake the salmon in a bowl with a fork. Add the cream cheese, lemon juice, onion, salt and liquid smoke and mix well. Chill, covered, for 2 to 10 hours.

Shape the salmon mixture into a log. Roll in a mixture of the pecans and parsley. Chill, wrapped in plastic wrap, for several hours. Serve with assorted party crackers.

Serves 10 to 12

SALMON SPREAD ELEGANTE

Here is a delicious appetizer for a group of four that is simple and quick to prepare at the last minute, as well as easy to transport and serve.

9 ounces smoked salmon
2 tablespoons chopped onion
2 tablespoons sour cream
1 tablespoon chopped fresh parsley

1 tablespoon chopped drained
  capers
1 tablespoon lemon juice
Party toast or sliced baguette

Chop the smoked salmon with a sharp knife. Combine the salmon, onion, sour cream, parsley, capers and lemon juice in a bowl and mix well. Spoon the salmon spread onto party toast squares or baguette slices.

Makes 1 1/4 cups

SYMPHONIES UNDER THE STARS

FIFTH WEEK AUGUST 5-7-8-9

OFFICIAL PROGRAM 1930   PRICE 10c

SOUPS, BREADS, AND SANDWICHES

AVOCADO BISQUE

A California summertime classic with velvety springtime overtones.

2 tablespoons butter

1/4 cup minced onion

2 tablespoons flour

3 cups chicken broth

1 tablespoon fresh lemon juice

1 tablespoon tarragon vinegar

1 tablespoon prepared horseradish, drained

1 garlic clove, crushed

1 teaspoon salt

1/4 teaspoon curry powder

1/4 teaspoon tarragon

Freshly ground pepper to taste

1 large ripe avocado, chopped

1 cup chicken broth

1 cup milk

1 cup light cream

Heat the butter in a 3-quart saucepan. Sauté the onion in the butter until tender but not brown. Stir in the flour. Add 3 cups broth, lemon juice, vinegar, horseradish, garlic, salt, curry powder, tarragon and pepper and mix well. Simmer, covered, for 10 minutes, stirring occasionally.

Process the avocado in a food processor or blender until puréed. Add 1 cup broth and process until blended. Stir the avocado purée into the soup. Add the milk and light cream. Bring to a boil; reduce the heat.

Simmer for 5 minutes, stirring occasionally. Transfer the soup to a bowl. Chill, covered, in the refrigerator. Ladle into soup bowls. You may serve hot but the flavor is richer if chilled before serving.

Serves 8

COLD CHERRY SOUP

3 cups cold water

1 cup sugar

1 cinnamon stick

4 cups fresh or canned sour cherries,
   pitted, chopped if desired

2 tablespoons cold water

1 tablespoon arrowroot or cornstarch

3/4 cup dry red wine

1/4 cup heavy cream (optional)

Combine 3 cups cold water, sugar and cinnamon stick in a 2-quart saucepan. Bring to a boil. Stir in the cherries; reduce the heat. Simmer, partially covered, over low heat for 35 minutes for fresh cherries or 10 minutes for canned cherries, stirring occasionally. Discard the cinnamon stick.

Combine 2 tablespoons cold water and arrowroot in a bowl and mix until of a pasty consistency. Whisk into the cherry mixture. Bring the soup almost to a boil, stirring constantly; reduce the heat.

Simmer for 2 minutes or until the mixture is clear and slightly thickened, stirring occasionally. Chill, covered, in the refrigerator. Stir in the wine. Ladle into soup bowls. Add a swirl of heavy cream to each bowl just before serving.

Serves 6

BLENDER STRAWBERRY AND WINE SOUP

2 cups strawberries

1 cup water

1/2 cup sugar

1 cup white wine

1 to 2 tablespoons lemon juice

1 tablespoon grated lemon zest

Sliced strawberries (optional)

Combine 2 cups strawberries, water and sugar in a blender container. Process until puréed. Stir in the wine, lemon juice and lemon zest. Chill, covered, in the refrigerator. Ladle into soup bowls. Garnish each serving with sliced strawberries.

Serves 4

CHILLED CREAM OF CUCUMBER SOUP WITH CURRY

Ken Frank, chef/owner of LaToque Restaurant located in Napa Valley and long-time friend of the Hollywood Bowl, contributed this lively cool soup recipe for a summer's day. Served hot, this soup has plenty of kick. But cold, the contrast between the spicy curry and the chilled cucumber is an invigorating surprise.

2 hothouse cucumbers

1 medium onion, thinly sliced

1/4 cup (1/2 stick) unsalted butter

1 cup water

2 tablespoons curry powder

Cayenne pepper to taste

Salt to taste

1 cup heavy cream, chilled

1/4 cup crème fraîche or sour cream

4 teaspoons chutney

Crushed red chiles (optional)

Cut the cucumbers lengthwise into halves and thinly slice each half. Sauté the onion in the butter in a cast-iron Dutch oven until golden brown. Stir in the cucumbers and water. Add the curry powder, cayenne pepper and salt and mix well. Bring to a boil; reduce the heat.

Simmer, partially covered, for 15 minutes, stirring occasionally. Remove from heat. Let stand until room temperature. Process the cucumber mixture in a blender or food processor until puréed. Strain into a bowl through a medium strainer. Do not use a fine strainer as the soup should have some body. Stir in the heavy cream. Chill, covered, in the refrigerator. Taste and adjust the seasonings. The soup will require more seasonings cold than hot.

Pour the crème fraîche into a plastic squeeze bottle. Ladle the soup into chilled soup bowls. Top each serving with a zigzag of the crème fraîche and 1 teaspoon of the chutney. Sprinkle with red chiles. Serve immediately.

Serves 4

JOACHIM SPLICHAL'S COLD SPRING PEA SOUP

3/4 cup plain yogurt

3/4 cup dried split green peas

1/4 cup (1/2 stick) unsalted butter

1/2 small yellow onion, coarsely
 chopped

1 small leek bulb, coarsely chopped

2 ribs celery, coarsely chopped

3 garlic cloves, crushed with
 chef's knife

1 sprig fresh thyme

1 slice apple-smoked bacon or other
 smoky bacon, coarsely chopped

1 quart Chicken Stock (page 33)

3 cups (about 1 pound) frozen
 green peas

Salt and freshly ground white pepper
 to taste

1/2 teaspoon coarsely cracked
 white pepper

18 sprigs mint, tops only

Chill 6 soup bowls and a soup tureen. Line a sieve with a double thickness of cheesecloth and spoon the yogurt into the sieve. Place the sieve over a bowl. Drain in the refrigerator for 8 to 10 hours. Sort and rinse the split peas. Combine with a generous amount of water in a bowl. Let stand for 8 to 10 hours; drain.

Heat the butter in a large saucepan over medium heat. Stir in the onion, leek, celery, garlic, thyme and bacon. Cook for 3 to 4 minutes or until the vegetables are tender, stirring occasionally. Stir in the split peas and stock. Bring just to a simmer.

Simmer, partially covered, over low heat for 45 to 50 minutes or until the peas are tender, stirring occasionally; remove the cover. Cool for 15 minutes. Stir in the frozen peas.

Process the soup in batches in a food processor fitted with a metal blade or a blender until puréed. Process each batch for an additional 3 to 4 minutes or until very smooth, scraping down the side of the bowl as necessary. For a perfectly smooth soup, push the purée through a fine strainer. Season with salt and freshly ground white pepper to taste.

Using 2 teaspoons, mold 3 small ovals of the strained yogurt and arrange in the bottom of one of the chilled soup bowls. Repeat the process for the remaining 5 bowls. Sprinkle lightly with 1/2 teaspoon coarsely cracked white pepper and arrange a mint sprig between each oval. Pour the soup into a chilled soup tureen. Ladle the soup into each bowl at the table.

Serves 6

CHICKEN STOCK

1 1/2 quarts water

5 pounds uncooked chicken carcasses, wings or assorted pieces

2 whole carrots

2 whole ribs celery

1 whole leek

1 medium yellow onion, peeled

1/2 unpeeled head garlic

10 white peppercorns, lightly crushed

1 sprig thyme

Combine the water and chicken pieces in a large stockpot. Bring to a slow simmer over medium heat. Skim the impurities from the surface with a large flat spoon. Stir in the carrots, celery, leek, onion, garlic, peppercorns and thyme. Simmer, partially covered, for 5 hours, adding additional water if the level of the liquid falls below the level of the bones; do not stir.

Strain the stock into a bowl through a strainer lined with a double thickness of moistened cheesecloth. Let stand until cool. Chill for 8 to 10 hours. Skim the fat from the top of the stock and discard. Use the stock as needed or freeze for future use. Double or triple this recipe if you have a large stockpot.

Makes 1 1/2 quarts

1922   *On Thursday, July 11, Dr. Alfred Hertz conducted the first Symphonies Under the Stars before a record audience of 5,000. Mary Pickford and Douglas Fairbanks were guests of Mrs. Hertz in the Hertz box. The third Bowl symphony concert, on the following Saturday, July 15, marked the date of Dr. Hertz' 50th birthday and also the Hertzes' eighth wedding anniversary. On this occasion, Mrs. Hertz attracted as much attention as the maestro by entering her box accompanied by matinee idol Rudolph Valentino.*

VICHYSSOISE

For an elegant treat, garnish with your favorite caviar.

3 tablespoons butter
3 medium leeks, trimmed, chopped
2 medium potatoes, peeled, chopped
4 cups chicken stock
1 cup heavy cream
1 cup milk
Salt and pepper to taste
Sprigs of fresh chives, dillweed or parsley (optional)

Heat the butter in a 3-quart saucepan. Stir in the leeks. Cook until tender, stirring occasionally. Stir in the potatoes and stock. Bring to a boil; reduce the heat.

Simmer, covered, for 30 minutes or until the potatoes are tender, stirring occasionally. Transfer the potato mixture to a blender or food processor container. Process until puréed.

Heat the heavy cream and milk in a saucepan. Stir the potato mixture into the cream mixture. Season with salt and pepper. Cook just until heated through, stirring occasionally. Cool slightly. Chill, covered, for 3 hours or longer. Ladle into soup bowls. Garnish each serving with sprigs of fresh chives, dillweed or parsley.

Serves 4 to 6

1922   The organizational road to Symphonies Under the Stars was paved by an often-fractious group of Hollywood real estate developers and businessmen. When funds ran out midway through the inaugural season, business minds proposed replacing the symphonic programs with cheaper band concerts. "Mother" Artie Mason Carter took the problem directly to the audience and raised enough money to see the season completed.

TOMATO, CRAB AND AVOCADO GAZPACHO

Joachim Splichal at Patina Restaurant gives this favorite summer soup extra color and flavor.

12 Roma tomatoes
1/4 cup coarsely chopped peeled English cucumber
1/4 cup finely chopped red onion
1/4 cup finely chopped celery
1/4 cup red bell pepper, roasted, peeled, seeded, diced
1 teaspoon finely minced garlic
2 teaspoons extra-virgin olive oil
2 teaspoons finely chopped Italian parsley
Lemon juice to taste
Coarse salt to taste
Freshly ground white pepper to taste
Cayenne pepper to taste
4 ounces lump crab meat, drained
1/2 avocado, chopped

Process the tomatoes in a food processor until puréed. Force the purée through a medium sieve, reserving the tomato juice and discarding the seeds and tomato peel.

Process the cucumber in a food processor until coarsely puréed. Combine the reserved tomato juice, cucumber purée, onion, celery, roasted red pepper and garlic in a bowl. Stir in the olive oil, parsley, lemon juice, salt, white pepper and cayenne pepper.

Chill, covered, in the refrigerator. Ladle into soup bowls. Top each serving with crab meat and chopped avocado.

Serves 4 to 6

COLD LEEK AND SUN-DRIED TOMATO SOUP

2 tablespoons olive oil

1 teaspoon chopped garlic

1 teaspoon chopped shallot

1 1/2 pounds leeks, tops removed, chopped

1/2 cup chopped sun-dried tomatoes

4 cups rich chicken stock

2 cups chopped canned tomatoes, drained

1 cup white wine

White pepper to taste

Chopped fresh parsley (optional)

Heat the olive oil in a stockpot for 1 minute. Sauté the garlic and shallot in the hot oil for 1 minute. Stir in the leeks and sun-dried tomatoes. Sauté for 1 minute. Remove the leek mixture to a bowl.

Combine the stock, canned tomatoes and wine in the stockpot and mix well. Bring to a boil; reduce the heat. Simmer for 20 minutes, stirring occasionally. Stir in the leek mixture. Let stand until cool.

Process the tomato mixture in a blender or food processor until puréed. Season with white pepper. Chill, covered, in the refrigerator. Ladle into soup bowls. Sprinkle each serving with chopped parsley.

Serves 6 to 8

1924   *Charles Toberman and E.N. Martin, early supporters of the Hollywood Bowl, were instrumental in having the Bowl property deeded to the County of Los Angeles, thus sparing the Bowl Association from paying taxes and ensuring a long-term lease with control of the Bowl's operations.*

SPICY BLACK BEAN SOUP

1/2 large onion

1/2 red bell pepper, cut into halves

1 small carrot, thickly sliced

5 garlic cloves, crushed

2 tablespoons canola oil

1 teaspoon cumin

1 teaspoon oregano

1 teaspoon paprika

3 (15-ounce) cans black beans, drained, rinsed

1 1/2 cups chicken broth

1/4 cup tomato paste

1 to 2 tablespoons chopped canned chipotle chiles with marinade

Salt to taste

1 avocado, chopped

1/4 cup chopped green onions

1/4 cup fresh cilantro leaves

Blue corn tortilla chips

Combine the onion, bell pepper, carrot and garlic in a food processor bowl. Pulse until the vegetables are coarsely chopped. Heat the canola oil in a large skillet. Stir in the chopped vegetables.

Cook, covered, for 10 minutes or until tender, stirring occasionally. Sprinkle with the cumin, oregano and paprika. Stir in the beans, broth and tomato paste. Simmer, covered, for 30 minutes, stirring occasionally. Stir in the undrained chipotle chiles. Taste and season with salt as needed.

Pour the soup into a wide-mouth thermos for transportation to your picnic. Ladle into 9-ounce tumblers at the picnic site and top each serving with chopped avocado, green onions and cilantro. Serve with blue corn tortilla chips. Rinse chopped avocado with hot water to prevent browning.

Serves 4 to 6

ROSEMARY CLOONEY'S CORN CHOWDER

3 ears of corn, shucked, silk removed

5 cups chicken stock

2 tablespoons butter

1 1/2 cups chopped onions

3/4 cup chopped celery

1/2 orange or yellow bell pepper, chopped

1 (4-ounce) can chopped green chiles, drained

1 bunch fresh tarragon

1 to 1 1/2 cups half-and-half

1/8 teaspoon sugar

Salt and pepper to taste

Cayenne pepper to taste

Cut the tops of the corn kernels with a sharp knife into a measuring cup, reserving the cobs. The corn should measure 2 1/2 cups. Combine the cobs and stock in a stockpot. Bring to a boil; reduce the heat. Simmer for 20 to 30 minutes; discard the cobs.

Heat the butter in a saucepan. Stir in the onions and celery. Cook over low heat for 2 to 3 minutes, stirring frequently. Add the onion mixture, bell pepper, green chiles and tarragon to the stock and mix well.

Simmer for 15 minutes, stirring occasionally. Stir in the corn, half-and-half, sugar, salt, pepper and cayenne pepper. Simmer for 2 minutes longer, stirring occasionally. Discard the tarragon stalks. Ladle into soup bowls.

Serves 6

SOUTHWESTERN CORN BREAD

The zesty flavor in an old favorite makes a salad meal more exciting.

1/2 cup canola oil or vegetable oil

1 cup buttermilk or yogurt

3 eggs

1 1/2 cups yellow or white cornmeal

1/2 cup flour

1/4 cup sugar

1 tablespoon baking powder

1 teaspoon salt

1 cup shredded Longhorn cheese

2 jalapeño chiles, seeded, finely chopped

Heat the canola oil in a glass loaf pan at 400 degrees for 10 minutes. Whisk the buttermilk and eggs in a bowl until blended. Combine the cornmeal, flour, sugar, baking powder and salt in a bowl and mix well. Stir in the egg mixture. Pour about 2/3 of the hot canola oil into the batter, leaving the remainder of the oil in the loaf pan. Fold in the cheese and jalapeño chiles.

Spoon the batter into the prepared loaf pan. Bake at 400 degrees for 25 minutes or until brown and crisp on top. Invert onto a wire rack. Slice and serve warm.

Serves 12

1924 *Famed coloratura soprano Amelita Galli-Curci, in a June off-season performance, "packed them in," singing without amplification to 21,873 listeners.*

BEARNAISE BREAD

1/2 cup sherry vinegar
1/2 cup dry vermouth
3 tablespoons minced shallots
2 tablespoons fresh tarragon leaves
1/2 teaspoon cracked pepper

1 1/2 cups (3 sticks) unsalted butter,
  cut into 1/2-inch slices
Salt to taste
1 baguette, cut into 1/4-inch slices

Combine the vinegar, vermouth, shallots, tarragon and cracked pepper in a saucepan. Cook over medium heat until the liquid is almost evaporated and the sauce is reduced, stirring occasionally. Remove from heat. Let stand until cool. Combine the cooled sauce and butter in a food processor bowl fitted with a steel blade. Process until smooth. Season with salt.

Spread 1 side of 10 slices of the bread with some of the béarnaise butter. Arrange the slices together to form a small loaf and wrap tightly in foil. Repeat the process with the remaining bread slices and remaining butter. Bake at 375 degrees for 15 minutes or until heated through.

Serves 12 to 15

ZUCCHINI COCONUT BREAD

3 cups flour
1 teaspoon each cinnamon, baking
  soda and baking powder
1 teaspoon salt
2 cups sugar
1 cup vegetable oil

3 eggs, beaten
2 teaspoons vanilla extract
3 cups grated zucchini
1 1/2 cups chopped walnuts
1 1/2 cups shredded coconut
1 cup golden raisins

Sift the flour, cinnamon, baking soda, baking powder and salt into a bowl and mix well. Stir in the sugar, oil, eggs and vanilla. Fold in the zucchini, walnuts, coconut and raisins.

Spoon the batter into 2 greased loaf pans. Bake at 350 degrees for about 50 minutes or until the loaves test done. Cool in pans for 10 minutes. Remove to a wire rack to cool completely. You may bake in muffin cups for about 30 minutes.

Makes 2 loaves

URBAN FOCACCIA

Freshly prepared pizza dough

1/4 cup olive oil

Coarse salt

Chopped fresh sage

Chopped fresh rosemary

Sliced Greek or niçoise olives

Thinly sliced onions

Grated Parmesan cheese or Romano
cheese

Pat the dough into a circle on a greased baking sheet. Drizzle with the olive oil and sprinkle with salt. Top with sage, rosemary, olives and onions or the toppings of your choice. Sprinkle with cheese.
Bake at 350 degrees for 30 minutes. You may substitute 1 prepared pizza shell for the pizza dough. Bake using package directions.

Serves 6 to 8

PITA CRISPS

This is an all-purpose crispy treat for picnics. Use the basic oil and garlic recipe for scooping up dips and the more flavorful ones as accompaniments for soups and salads.

6 (6-inch) pita bread rounds, split

1/4 cup olive oil

1/2 teaspoon herbs such as basil,
thyme, oregano or a combination
(optional)

1 garlic clove, crushed or minced

1/3 cup grated Parmesan cheese or
shredded sharp Cheddar cheese
(optional)

Cut each round into 4 wedges with a knife or kitchen shears. Combine the olive oil, herbs and garlic in a bowl and mix well. Brush the split sides of the wedges with the olive oil mixture. Sprinkle with the cheese. Arrange the wedges oil side up in a single layer on a baking sheet. Bake at 400 degrees for 5 to 10 minutes or until golden brown and crisp. Serve warm or at room temperature, allowing 3 to 4 pita crisps per guest. Store in an airtight container for future use.

Makes 4 dozen pita crisps

PATAFLA SANDWICH

This combination of bread and salad is a favorite Hollywood Bowl picnic dish.
Prepare one day in advance so the flavors have a chance to blend.

4 "hero" size French or Italian rolls
4 ripe tomatoes, peeled
1 large onion, finely chopped
2 ounces green olives, chopped
2 ounces black olives, chopped
2 green bell peppers, chopped
2 ounces gherkins, chopped
2 ounces capers, drained
Olive oil to taste
$1/8$ teaspoon paprika
Salt and freshly ground pepper to taste

Cut the rolls lengthwise into halves. Remove the centers carefully, leaving a shell. Crumble the bread from the centers.

Combine the tomatoes, onion, olives, bell peppers, pickles and capers in a bowl and mix well. Add the reserved bread crumbs to the tomato mixture, adding a little olive oil for the desired consistency and taste. Stir in the paprika and season with salt and pepper.

Spoon the tomato mixture into the bread shells and press firmly. Press the halves together and wrap tightly in foil to form 4 sandwiches. Chill for 8 to 10 hours. Slice at the picnic site.

Makes 4 sandwiches

PAN BEIGNET

This sandwich is very traditional picnic fare in the South of France and the Riviera.

1 large loaf French bread
Olivada (kalamata olive paste)
1 cup arugula
2 (7-ounce) cans white tuna, drained
$1/2$ cup mayonnaise
3 tablespoons capers
2 tablespoons lemon juice
2 or 3 large tomatoes, thinly sliced
1 red onion, thinly sliced

Cut the bread loaf horizontally into halves. Remove the centers carefully, leaving a $1/2$-inch shell. Discard the bread center; use in another recipe or freeze for future use. Spread the olive paste over the bottom and up the side of the bottom bread shell. Layer with the arugula.

Combine the tuna, mayonnaise, capers and lemon juice in a bowl and mix well. Spread the tuna mixture over the arugula. Arrange the sliced tomatoes and sliced onion over the tuna mixture. Top with the remaining bread shell and wrap in heavy-duty foil. Chill for 24 hours or longer. To serve, cut diagonally into quarters.

Serves 4

1925 *Conductor Ethel Leginska was an early and dramatic example of Women's Lib. She was infuriated by a critic's remark that she "...should stick to the innocuous composers..." and programmed Beethoven's Seventh Symphony for her appearance. She electrified the audience but enraged the 90 rebellious men in the orchestra. She proved herself a brilliant conductor, and, remembering her virtuosity, the orchestra treated a later woman conductor, Antonia Brico, with more respect.*

WRAP SANDWICHES

The possibilities are infinite...we offer a few guidelines and suggestions.

The Wrap

Lavash, flour tortilla or flexible thin flat bread of your choice

The Spread

Butter, margarine, softened cream cheese or sour cream with
horseradish, mayonnaise, mustard or curry powder and
lemon juice (with or without finely chopped herbs)

The Protein

Thinly sliced cold cuts of roast beef, turkey, pork, chicken, salami,
liverwurst, ham or smoked salmon; cheeses such as Jack cheese,
Cheddar cheese, Swiss cheese, Havarti cheese or Gruyère cheese

The Veggies

Thinly sliced, chopped or minced tomatoes, avocados, mushrooms,
cucumbers, radishes, onions, spinach, sprouts, bell peppers, olives,
chopped nuts or shredded lettuce

To assemble, lay the flexible thin bread of choice on a cutting board. Cover with the spread. Arrange the protein and vegetables over the spread, leaving a $1/2$-inch border around the edge. Roll to enclose the filling and wrap tightly in plastic wrap. Chill for 2 to 10 hours. Slice as desired.

To prepare a wrap without bread, spread 2 thin slices of roast beef with mustard and/or horseradish. Roll around a dill pickle approximately $1/4$ inch in diameter and tie with fresh chives.

Variable servings

Side Salads

BEACH BROCCOLI SALAD

Joan Stubbs, the Hollywood Bowl cookbook co-chairman from 1994 to 1999, contributed this recipe.

3 stalks fresh broccoli, chopped

8 slices bacon, crisp-cooked, crumbled

1 cup golden raisins

1/4 cup chopped red onion

1 cup chopped cashews or pecans

Red Wine Vinaigrette (below)

Drop the broccoli into boiling water in a saucepan. Boil for 2 to 3 minutes to bring out the color and eliminate the bitter taste; drain. Cool to room temperature.

Combine the broccoli, bacon, raisins, onion and cashews in a salad bowl and mix well. Add the Red Wine Vinaigrette and toss to coat. Serve chilled or at room temperature.

You may prepare 1 day in advance and store, covered, in the refrigerator, adding the bacon and cashews just before serving to prevent them from becoming soggy.

Serves 6 to 8

RED WINE VINAIGRETTE

1 cup mayonnaise

3 tablespoons light brown sugar

2 tablespoons red wine vinegar

1 tablespoon curry powder

2 tablespoons mango chutney (optional)

Combine the mayonnaise, brown sugar, vinegar, curry powder and chutney in a small bowl and mix well.

Serves 6 to 8

ARMENIAN CABBAGE SLAW

1 medium head cabbage (about 2 pounds)

3 tablespoons olive oil or vegetable oil

3 tablespoons lemon juice

1^1/2 tablespoons white wine vinegar

1^1/2 tablespoons water

^{1}/2 teaspoon ground pepper

^{1}/2 teaspoon sugar

1 medium red onion, cut into 4 wedges

^{1}/2 cup chopped fresh mint leaves, or ^{1}/4 cup dried mint

Remove the large outer leaves of the cabbage. Rinse the leaves, wrap in paper towels and place in a sealable plastic bag. Chill until ready to serve slaw.

Thinly shred the remaining cabbage into a large bowl. Whisk the olive oil, lemon juice, vinegar, water, pepper and sugar in a small bowl. Add to the cabbage and toss to coat. Finely chop 3 of the onion wedges and add to the cabbage mixture along with the mint and mix well.

Arrange the reserved cabbage leaves in a wide shallow salad bowl so the edges of the leaves are above the rim of the bowl. Spoon the slaw into the prepared bowl. Thinly slice the remaining onion wedge and scatter over the top of the slaw. You may prepare the slaw up to 1 day in advance and store, covered with plastic wrap, in the refrigerator. Do not sprinkle with the onion until just before serving.

Serves 8 to 10

1925   *Repertoire was hardly provincial when young Fritz Reiner programmed Stravinsky, Honnegger, and Falla, and Sir Henry Wood offered Holst, Vaughan Williams, and Turina.*

RED AND WHITE CABBAGE SALAD

2 cups shredded red cabbage

2 cups shredded white cabbage

2 garlic cloves, crushed

1 ounce anchovies, mashed, or
   to taste

1/4 cup olive oil

1 tablespoon white wine vinegar

1/8 teaspoon lemon juice

Salt and freshly ground pepper
   to taste

Place the red and white cabbage in 2 separate bowls. Mash the garlic and anchovies together in a bowl with a fork. Whisk in the olive oil, vinegar, lemon juice, salt and pepper.

Divide the dressing into 2 equal portions. Toss 1 portion of the dressing with each bowl of cabbage. Mound the white cabbage in the center of a shallow serving bowl. Arrange the red cabbage around the white cabbage.

Serves 4

MIXED GREENS WITH TOMATO VINAIGRETTE

1 medium tomato, peeled

5 tablespoons extra-virgin olive oil

1 tablespoon red wine vinegar

1 tablespoon lemon juice

1 tablespoon coarse-grain
   Dijon mustard

1 1/2 teaspoons crushed garlic

1 1/2 teaspoons chopped fresh chives

1/2 teaspoon herbes de Provence, or
   a combination of dried thyme, basil
   and oregano

8 cups lightly packed mixed salad
   greens (curly endive, radicchio and
   arugula)

Combine the tomato, olive oil, vinegar, lemon juice, Dijon mustard, garlic, chives and herbes de Provence in a food processor or blender container. Process until smooth.

Place the salad greens in a medium salad bowl. Add 1/3 to 1/2 cup of the vinaigrette and toss to mix. Serve immediately.

Serves 4

FIELD GREENS AND RASPBERRY SALAD

Use fresh blueberries instead of raspberries for variety, or try feta cheese instead of bleu cheese.

4 cups torn baby lettuce
2 thin slices red or sweet onion, chopped
1 cup fresh raspberries
1/2 cup pecans or walnuts, toasted
1/4 cup crumbled bleu cheese (optional)
Raspberry Vinaigrette (below)

Mix the lettuce, onion, raspberries, pecans and bleu cheese in a salad bowl. Add the Raspberry Vinaigrette and toss to coat. Spoon the salad equally onto 4 chilled salad plates. Garnish with extra raspberries if desired.

Serves 4

RASPBERRY VINAIGRETTE

2 tablespoons walnut oil
2 tablespoons raspberry vinegar
1 tablespoon olive oil
1 tablespoon honey
Salt and pepper to taste

Combine the walnut oil, vinegar, olive oil, honey, salt and pepper in a jar with a tight-fitting lid; seal tightly. Shake to mix.

Serves 4

BABY SPINACH SALAD

2 bunches baby spinach, stems
   removed
6 radishes, cut into halves, cut into
   quarters

1 large avocado, chopped
1/4 cup chopped green onions
1/4 cup crumbled crisp-cooked bacon
Mustard Vinaigrette (below)

Combine the spinach, radishes, avocado, green onions and bacon in a salad bowl and mix gently. Add the Mustard Vinaigrette just before serving and toss to coat.

Serves 6

MUSTARD VINAIGRETTE

2 tablespoons white wine vinegar
2 tablespoons minced fresh parsley
  (optional)
2 teaspoons Dijon mustard

1/2 teaspoon sugar
1/4 teaspoon salt
1/4 teaspoon freshly ground pepper
1/3 cup extra-virgin olive oil

Combine the vinegar, parsley, Dijon mustard, sugar, salt and pepper in a bowl and mix well. Add the olive oil gradually, whisking constantly until thickened.

Serves 6

1925 *Eugene Goossens described his Bowl experience most poetically, saying, "The sensation of conducting a fine orchestra under that marvelous blue vault studded with blazing stars, with an audience of 20,000 to 30,000 thronging the darkness of the hillsides, remains unforgettable and indescribable."*

51

ROSEMARY CLOONEY'S SUMMER SALAD

1 bunch watercress
3 or 4 heads endive, torn into bite-size pieces
4 plum tomatoes, cut into quarters
2 hard-cooked eggs, coarsely chopped
1 small can julienned beets, drained
Spicy Balsamic Vinaigrette (below)

Remove the watercress leaves from the stalks, discarding the stalks. Combine the watercress leaves, endive, tomatoes, eggs and beets in a salad bowl and mix gently. Add the Spicy Balsamic Vinaigrette just before serving and toss to coat.

Serves 4 to 6

SPICY BALSAMIC VINAIGRETTE

1/4 cup extra-virgin olive oil
1/4 cup balsamic vinegar
2 garlic cloves, crushed
1 tablespoon bottled chili sauce
1/2 teaspoon soy sauce
Freshly ground pepper to taste

Combine the olive oil, vinegar, garlic, chili sauce, soy sauce and pepper in a jar with a tight-fitting lid; seal tightly. Shake to mix.

Serves 4 to 6

SUMMER SALAD WITH PECANS AND PEARS

4 medium ripe pears, thinly sliced

2 teaspoons lemon juice

8 cups torn salad greens

2/3 cup pecan halves, toasted

1/2 cup fresh raspberries

1/3 cup crumbled feta cheese or
  bleu cheese

Fresh Raspberry Vinaigrette (below)

Toss the pears with the lemon juice in a salad bowl. Add the salad greens, pecans and raspberries to the salad bowl and mix gently. Sprinkle with the feta cheese. Drizzle the Fresh Raspberry Vinaigrette over the salad just before serving.

Serves 6 to 8

FRESH RASPBERRY VINAIGRETTE

2 tablespoons fresh raspberries

3/4 cup olive oil or vegetable oil

3 tablespoons cider vinegar

2 tablespoons plus 1 teaspoon sugar

1/4 to 1/2 teaspoon pepper

Press the raspberries through a sieve into a bowl, reserving the juice and discarding the seeds. Whisk the reserved juice, olive oil, vinegar, sugar and pepper in a bowl until blended.

Serves 6 to 8

1926 *Percy Grainger, the famous Australian composer and conductor, announced from the stage his engagement to Swedish poet Viola Strom. He had composed a tribute titled "To a Nordic Princess" to his betrothed and wanted to play it at one of his concerts. Business manager Raymond Brite suggested, "Better still, why not be married in the Bowl?" So, after the August 9 concert, Grainger and Miss Strom were married before an audience of 15,000.*

AVOCADO, CARROT AND ORANGE SALAD

2 tablespoons seedless raisins

1 tablespoon orange-flavor liqueur or warm water

3/4 cup orange juice

1 tablespoon grated orange zest

1/2 teaspoon salt

1/8 teaspoon crushed red pepper

1/8 teaspoon finely grated fresh gingerroot

2 cups coarsely grated carrots

1 large ripe avocado, chilled, cut into 8 wedges

Soak the raisins in the liqueur in a bowl for 20 minutes; drain. Combine the orange juice, orange zest, salt, red pepper and gingerroot in a deep bowl and mix well. Add the carrots and stir until thoroughly moistened. Chill, covered, for 2 hours or longer.

Remove the carrots to a shallow serving bowl using a slotted spoon. Sprinkle with the raisins. Arrange the avocado wedges in a pinwheel around the edge of the carrots.

Serves 4 to 6

1927   *Dance, drama, and community events held special places on Bowl agendas: Dr. Alfred Hertz conducted a program featuring dancers Ruth St. Denis and Ted Shawn, Reginald de Koven's operetta* Robin Hood *was produced, and a group of Native Americans leased the Bowl for intertribal ceremonies. By then, the amphitheater had become a summer entertainment mecca for Los Angeles.*

ROASTED BEET SALAD

Not your grandmother's beet salad! Roast the beets and taste the difference.

6 fresh young beets
1/2 cup olive oil
1/4 cup wine vinegar
1/2 teaspoon salt
1/2 teaspoon pepper
1/2 teaspoon grated orange or lemon zest
Mixed salad greens
Sliced hard-cooked eggs

Cut the green tops off the beets to within 1 inch of the beets. Wrap the beets in foil. Bake at 400 degrees for 45 minutes or until tender. Cool slightly. Peel the beets, slice and place in a bowl.

Whisk the olive oil, vinegar, salt, pepper and orange or lemon zest in a bowl until mixed. Add the dressing to the warm beets and gently toss to coat. Spoon the beets onto a serving platter lined with mixed salad greens. Garnish with sliced hard-cooked eggs.

Serves 4

CUCUMBER AND JICAMA SALAD

1 1/2 cups coarsely grated peeled cucumbers

1 cup plain yogurt

1 1/2 cups coarsely grated peeled jicama

3 tablespoons chopped green onions

1 tablespoon chopped fresh dillweed

3 tablespoons chopped fresh Italian parsley

4 tablespoons raisins

4 tablespoons pistachios, toasted, coarsely chopped

Salt and pepper to taste

Drain the cucumbers in a colander for 10 to 15 minutes. Discard any water in the yogurt.

Combine the cucumbers, jicama, green onions and dillweed in a bowl and mix well. Stir in 2 tablespoons of the parsley, 2 tablespoons of the raisins and 2 tablespoons of the pistachios. Add the yogurt, salt and pepper and mix well.

Chill, covered, until serving time. Sprinkle with the remaining 1 tablespoon parsley, remaining 2 tablespoons raisins and remaining 2 tablespoons pistachios just before serving.

Serves 4

1927-1929 *After four years of performances under a canvas roof and another of using a wooden shell, in 1927 Lloyd Wright (son of Frank Lloyd Wright) designed a pyramid-shaped wooden shell, which was used for only one season. In 1928, he designed a "streamline moderne" shell formed of nine concentric segmental arches that could be "tuned" panel by panel. In 1929, a shell made of transite (a cement and asbestos mixture) was designed by Allied Architects and the engineering firm of Elliott, Bowen and Walz.*

ASIAN SESAME EGGPLANT SALAD

1 1/2 pounds small Japanese eggplant

Vegetable oil

1 1/2 tablespoons sesame seeds

2 tablespoons soy sauce

2 tablespoons sesame oil

1 1/2 tablespoons tahini (sesame paste)

1 tablespoon Chinese black vinegar or balsamic vinegar

1 tablespoon minced green onions

2 teaspoons sugar

1 1/2 teaspoons crushed garlic

1 1/2 teaspoons minced green ginger

1/4 to 1/2 teaspoon cayenne pepper, chili oil or chili paste

Cut the eggplant horizontally into halves. Brush the cut sides with vegetable oil. Arrange the eggplant cut side up on a rack in a roasting pan. Broil for 10 to 15 minutes or until brown and tender. Let stand until cool. Arrange the eggplant cut side up in a serving dish.

Toast the sesame seeds in a skillet over medium heat until golden brown, stirring occasionally. Whisk the soy sauce, sesame oil, tahini, vinegar, green onions, sugar, garlic, green ginger and cayenne pepper in a bowl until mixed. Drizzle over the eggplant and sprinkle with the sesame seeds.

Serves 4 to 6

TOSSED SPICY PEPPER AND SNOW PEA SALAD

1 tablespoon canola oil

2 teaspoons sesame oil

3 medium red bell peppers, cut lengthwise into 3/4-inch strips

6 ounces fresh snow peas, trimmed

1 tablespoon rice wine or sherry

2 tablespoons soy sauce

2 teaspoons crushed garlic

1 teaspoon sugar

1 teaspoon sesame oil

1/2 to 1 teaspoon cayenne pepper, chili oil or chili paste

Heat a wok or deep skillet. Add the canola oil and 2 teaspoons sesame oil. Heat just to the smoking point. Stir-fry the bell peppers and snow peas in the hot oil for 30 seconds. Stir in the rice wine. Stir-fry for 30 seconds longer. Remove the bell pepper mixture to a bowl.

Mix the soy sauce, garlic, sugar, 1 teaspoon sesame oil and cayenne pepper in a bowl. Add to the wok. Cook for 30 seconds, stirring frequently. Drizzle the soy sauce mixture over the bell pepper mixture and toss to coat. May be served chilled or at room temperature.

Serves 4

BLEU CHEESE POTATO SALAD

2 pounds small new red potatoes (about 16 potatoes), cut into quarters

1/4 cup extra-virgin olive oil

1/4 cup white wine vinegar

Salt and freshly ground pepper to taste

1/4 cup chopped red onion

1/2 cup chopped fresh parsley

4 ounces bleu cheese, or to taste

Steam the potatoes for 10 to 15 minutes or until tender but firm; drain. Remove the potatoes to a bowl. Pour the olive oil and vinegar over the potatoes. Sprinkle with salt and pepper. Add the onion and gently toss.

Let stand until cool. Stir in the parsley and bleu cheese. Serve at room temperature.

Serves 6

1928 *Italian conductor Bernardino Molinari spoke little English, but his description of the Bowl, translated from the Italian, is eloquent indeed: "No conductor dares play down or program down to a Hollywood Bowl audience. They are neither bored by the classics nor shocked by the moderns....Most of all, they demand quality throughout, and while they share with all Americans the love for the spectacular, they refuse to accept it as a substitute for art. Nowhere else in the world can such a combination be found: a vast natural auditorium, an earnest, intelligent, sympathetic audience...a rich and generous city."*

GARLICKY NEW POTATO SALAD

1 1/2 pounds new red potatoes
4 large unpeeled garlic cloves
1 tablespoon olive oil
1/4 teaspoon salt
4 sprigs of rosemary
1 tablespoon white wine vinegar

2 teaspoons Dijon mustard
1/4 teaspoon salt
Pepper to taste
3 tablespoons olive oil
2 green onions, thinly sliced

Cut the new potatoes into 1 1/2-inch pieces. Combine the garlic, 1 tablespoon olive oil and 1/4 teaspoon salt in a bowl and mix well. Add the potatoes and toss to coat. Arrange the potato mixture in a single layer in a roasting pan lined with foil. Top with the sprigs of rosemary. Roast at 450 degrees for 30 to 40 minutes, stirring occasionally. Discard the rosemary and remove the potatoes and garlic to a bowl.

Whisk the vinegar, Dijon mustard, 1/4 teaspoon salt and pepper in a bowl. Whisk in 3 tablespoons olive oil. Squeeze the roasted garlic into the olive oil mixture and mix well, discarding the skins. Drizzle the dressing over the potatoes and toss until coated. Sprinkle with the green onions. Serve at room temperature.

Serves 4

1929 *Aaron Copland came to the Bowl to play the West Coast premiere of his jazz-influenced Piano Concerto. "At the rehearsals the musicians actually hissed," he recalled in his autobiography, "and the conductor, Albert Coates, was distraught. 'Boys, boys,' Coates pleaded, 'he's one of us.'"*

RICE SALAD

1 cup mayonnaise

1 envelope Italian salad dressing mix

3 cups cooked rice

1 1/2 cups drained cooked green peas

1 cup cubed Cheddar cheese

1 cup grated carrots

1/4 cup chopped fresh chives

1/4 cup chopped pimentos

Combine the mayonnaise and dressing mix in a bowl and mix well. Combine the rice, green peas, cheese, carrots, chives and pimentos in a bowl and mix gently. Add the mayonnaise mixture and gently toss until coated.

Serves 6

TABBOULEH

2 cups fine cracked wheat
   (bulgur)

1 cup ice water

2 cups minced fresh parsley

1 cup finely chopped green onions

4 to 6 medium tomatoes, chopped

3/4 cup lemon juice

3/4 cup olive oil

3 tablespoons minced fresh mint, or
   1 tablespoon crushed dried mint

1 teaspoon salt

1/2 teaspoon ground pepper

Paprika to taste

1/4 cup olive oil

Romaine leaves

Armenian thin bread or pita bread

Combine the cracked wheat and ice water in a bowl and mix well. Chill, covered, for 1 hour. Stir in the parsley, green onions, tomatoes, lemon juice, 3/4 cup olive oil, mint, salt, pepper and paprika.

Chill, covered, for 1 hour. Stir in 1/4 cup olive oil just before serving. Spoon the tabbouleh into a deep serving bowl. Garnish with romaine and serve with Armenian thin bread. You may serve in small individual dishes lined with lettuce, garnishing with sprigs of fresh parsley.

You may prepare up to 1 week in advance and store, covered, in the refrigerator. Vary the amounts of the vegetables according to your taste. If the salad is too dry due to the quality of the tomatoes, add a small amount of tomato juice.

Serves 8 to 10

RIBBON SALAD

*This is a most eye-catching salad when unmolded or presented in clear glass.
Use colors of your choice...the flavors will blend.*

4 (3-ounce) packages fruit-flavor gelatin
4 cups boiling water
1 cup sour cream or cream cheese

Dissolve 1 package of the gelatin in 1 cup of the boiling water in a heatproof bowl. Pour 2/3 of the gelatin into an 8×12-inch dish. Chill until firm. Whisk the remaining gelatin with enough of the sour cream to measure 2/3 cup. Pour over the prepared layer. Chill until firm. Repeat the process with the remaining gelatin, remaining boiling water and remaining sour cream. The dish should hold 8 to 10 layers.

   Use different colors for each layer if desired or repeat the same color. For Christmas, use red and green alternately in a tree-shape mold. For a baby shower, use pastel colors. For the Fourth of July, use red, unflavored gelatin mixed with sour cream and blue. Or make a rainbow. The choices are endless.

Serves 10 to 12

1933   *Despite the Great Depression, between the Hertz years and the beginning of World War II, there was a golden era of dance, opera, and innovative events. Those were the years of Otto Klemperer, Bruno Walter, Lili Pons, Kirsten Flagstad, Agnes de Mille, Lawrence Tibbett, Paul Robeson, and the Ballet Russe de Monte Carlo.*

Hollywood Bowl *Magazine*

SEVENTH WEEK
august 26, 28, 30 - 1952

25¢

Selling Price . . .2427
Tax 0073

Total 2500

symphonies under the stars
hollywood bowl pops

ENTREE SALADS

DOLORES HOPE'S ANTIPASTO SALAD

This can be served as a first course salad or even as a main dish. Serve with hot crusty bread.

1 head iceberg lettuce, chilled, torn
    into bite-size pieces
Black olives, chilled, drained
Pimentos, drained, slivered
Garbanzo beans, chilled, drained
Genovese salami, cut into slivers
Shredded mozzarella cheese
Marinated artichoke hearts, chilled,
    drained

Mild pickled Italian chiles, drained
    (pepperoncini)
Celery hearts and tops, finely
    chopped
Salt and coarsely ground pepper
Wine vinegar
Olive oil

Arrange a bed of lettuce in a chilled salad bowl. Top with the olives, pimentos, garbanzo beans, salami, cheese, artichokes, chiles and celery. Take the salad to the table untossed to show off the colorful arrangement. Sprinkle with salt and pepper, drizzle with wine vinegar and gently toss. Add olive oil and toss to coat. Use approximately 3 parts olive oil to 1 part vinegar.

Serves 6 to 8

1934   *In September, under the auspices of the California Festival Association, the Bowl presented Max Reinhardt's production of A Midsummer Night's Dream, with Olivia de Havilland as Hermia and Mickey Rooney as Puck. The shell was removed and tons of earth brought in for the forest setting, and the orchestra played the Mendelssohn incidental music on a platform to the right, camouflaged by a barrier of trees. In response to popular demand, the performance was extended from four to eight nights. People marveled at the procession of the Wedding March, which wound through the hills with lighted torches.*

HENRY WINKLER'S MEXICAN SALAD

This is a fine entrée for the vegetarians at your picnic.

1 large head romaine, torn into
   1/2-inch pieces
8 ounces sharp Cheddar cheese,
   shredded
2 (4-ounce) cans sliced black olives,
   drained
3 large tomatoes, chopped

1 (4-ounce) can diced green chiles,
   drained
1 large red onion, chopped
Green Chile Dressing (below)
1 (10-ounce) package tortilla chips,
   broken
2 avocados, chopped

Toss the romaine, cheese, olives, tomatoes, green chiles and onion in a salad bowl. Add the Green Chile Dressing just before serving and toss to coat. Top with the tortilla chips and avocados.

Serves 8 to 10

GREEN CHILE DRESSING

1 1/2 cups mayonnaise
1 (7-ounce) can green chile salsa

1/3 cup ketchup
1/2 teaspoon chili powder

Combine the mayonnaise, salsa, ketchup and chili powder in a bowl and mix well. Chill, covered, in the refrigerator.

Serves 8 to 10

1936 *Coloratura soprano Lily Pons holds the Bowl's all-time attendance record of 26,410. On Friday, August 7, patrons began arriving as early as 1:00 p.m., carrying picnic baskets and reading material to while away the time before the ticket gates opened. Miss Pons' accompanying conductor was André Kostelanetz, her fiancé and later her husband.*

WARM ROAST BEEF AND POTATO SALAD

This is simple French country food...an ideal summer salad and an excellent way to use leftover roast beef. Ken Frank, chef/owner of LaToque Restaurant in Napa Valley, contributed this recipe.

Salt and freshly ground pepper
   to taste

1 pound top sirloin

Vegetable oil

4 medium long white potatoes

8 large butterhead lettuce leaves

2/3 cup Crème Fraîche (below)

1 red bell pepper, julienned

1 small red onion, julienned

1 tablespoon Pommery mustard

2 teaspoons sherry wine vinegar

1 bunch chives, finely minced

Sprinkle salt and pepper generously over the surface of the beef. Heat a small amount of oil in a Dutch oven over high heat. Sear the beef on all sides in the hot oil. Bake at 450 degrees for 20 minutes for rare, turning once. To test the degree of doneness, pierce the center of the beef with a skewer or the tines of a fork. Wait 5 seconds, remove the skewer and immediately touch the tip to your lower lip. If the skewer is slightly warm, the beef will be rare. Remove the beef from the oven.

Combine the potatoes and salt enough cold water to cover in a saucepan. Bring to a boil; reduce the heat. Simmer for 20 minutes or until the potatoes are tender; drain. Cool slightly. Peel and cut into 1/2-inch pieces. Chop the beef into 1/2-inch pieces. Line 4 plates with the lettuce leaves.

Bring the Crème Fraîche, potatoes, bell pepper and onion to a boil in a sauté pan. Stir in the remaining ingredients. Adjust seasonings. Remove from heat. Add the beef; toss until warm. (Cooking the beef further will make it tough.) Spoon the mixture onto the lettuce-lined plates. Serve immediately.

Serves 4

CREME FRAICHE

Buttermilk

Heavy cream

Mix 1 part buttermilk to 4 parts heavy cream in a bowl. Let stand at room temperature for 8 hours. Chill, covered, for 8 to 10 hours to thicken. May be stored in the refrigerator for 10 to 14 days. If you don't have time to make crème fraîche, you can use Devon cream or sour cream instead.

CHINESE CHICKEN SALAD FROM MICHAEL TILSON THOMAS

The most requested recipe from the 1984 Hollywood Bowl cookbook.

Salad

4 chicken breasts

1 head iceberg lettuce, torn into
   bite-size pieces

1 bunch green onions, thinly sliced

1/4 cup sesame seeds, toasted

1/4 to 1/2 cup slivered almonds,
   toasted

1 package won ton noodles, cut into
   4 to 6 strips, deep-fried

Sauce

2 tablespoons cornstarch

3/4 cup water

1 cup vinegar

6 tablespoons sugar

2 teaspoons soy sauce

Sesame oil to taste

For the salad, arrange the chicken in a single layer in a baking pan. Bake at 350 degrees for 45 minutes. Shred the chicken, discarding the skin and bones. Place the lettuce and green onions in a large salad bowl. Add the chicken and gently toss. Add the sesame seeds, almonds and won ton strips just before serving and toss.

For the sauce, place the cornstarch in a small bowl. Add the water gradually, stirring constantly. Combine the vinegar, sugar, soy sauce and sesame oil in a saucepan and mix well. Stir in the cornstarch mixture.

Bring to a boil, stirring constantly; reduce the heat. Simmer until thickened and clear, stirring frequently. Drizzle over the salad and toss to coat.

Serves 6 to 8

1937 *Two months after George Gershwin's death, the Bowl held a postseason Gershwin memorial concert, featuring many artists who had been associated with the young American composer, including Fred Astaire, Al Jolson, and Oscar Levant. Ever since, special Gershwin programs have been part of the Bowl season.*

ORIENTAL CHICKEN AND NOODLE SALAD

1 (2¹/2- to 3-pound) chicken, cut up
1 cup dry white wine
¹/2 cup water
4 (quarter-size) slices gingerroot
2 large garlic cloves
¹/2 teaspoon salt
12 ounces oriental-style dry noodles

1¹/2 to 2 tablespoons sesame oil
8 ounces jicama, julienned
1 large red bell pepper, julienned
6 large green onions, thinly sliced
¹/3 cup chopped fresh cilantro
Ginger Sesame Dressing (below)
³/4 cup almond slivers, toasted

Arrange the chicken in a single layer in a large skillet. Add the wine, water, gingerroot, garlic and salt. Bring to a boil; reduce the heat. Simmer, covered, for 25 minutes or until the chicken is cooked through, turning once; drain. Let stand until cool. Shred the chicken into bite-size pieces, discarding the skin, fat and bones.

Cook the noodles using package directions until al dente. Drain and rinse in cold water. Toss the noodles with the sesame oil in a bowl until coated. Add the jicama, bell pepper, green onions, half the cilantro and half the chicken to the noodles and mix well. Add just enough of the Ginger Sesame Dressing to taste and gently toss. Arrange the remaining chicken, remaining cilantro and almonds over the top of the salad. Serve with the remaining Ginger Sesame Dressing.

Serves 4 to 6

GINGER SESAME DRESSING

¹/3 cup vegetable oil
¹/4 cup seasoned rice vinegar
8 (¹/2-inch) cubes peeled gingerroot
1 tablespoon soy sauce

1 large garlic clove, cut into halves
1¹/2 teaspoons sesame oil
¹/4 teaspoon chile flakes

Combine the oil, vinegar, gingerroot, soy sauce, garlic, sesame oil and chile flakes in a blender or food processor container. Process until smooth. You may prepare 1 day in advance and store, covered, in the refrigerator.

Serves 4 to 6

GREEK SALAD WITH GRILLED CHICKEN

4 boneless skinless chicken breasts

Mint Dressing (below)

1 head romaine, torn

1 head iceberg lettuce, torn

1 cup finely crumbled feta cheese

1 cup kalamata olives

2 large tomatoes, chopped

2 cucumbers, chopped

1 red onion, chopped

Arrange the chicken in a single layer in a dish. Pour half the Mint Dressing over the chicken, turning to coat. Marinate, covered, in the refrigerator for 8 to 10 hours, turning occasionally. Drain, reserving the marinade.

Grill the chicken over high heat until cooked through, turning and basting with the reserved marinade occasionally. Cool slightly. Chill, covered, in the refrigerator.

Combine the romaine, iceberg lettuce, feta cheese, olives, tomatoes, cucumbers and onion in a salad bowl and mix well. Cut the chilled chicken into strips and add to the salad. Drizzle with the remaining Mint Dressing and toss to coat.

Serves 8 to 10

MINT DRESSING

2 cups extra-virgin olive oil

Juice of 3 large lemons

2 shallots, minced

2 tablespoons minced fresh mint

1 tablespoon minced fresh oregano

Freshly ground pepper to taste

Combine the olive oil, lemon juice, shallots, mint, oregano and pepper in a jar with a tight-fitting lid; seal tightly. Shake to mix.

Serves 8 to 10

GRILLED CHICKEN, WILD RICE AND MANGO SALAD

Chicken

1 pound boneless skinless chicken
    breasts
1/4 cup packed light brown sugar
2 tablespoons each rice wine vinegar
    and soy sauce
2 teaspoons vegetable oil
2 teaspoons grated orange zest
2 teaspoons minced gingerroot
2 garlic cloves, minced
1/4 teaspoon pepper

Salad

1 1/2 cups wild rice
2 ripe mangoes, peeled, cut into
    3/4-inch pieces
1 cup grated carrots
1/2 cup chopped fresh cilantro
Salt to taste
Rice Wine Vinaigrette (below)
Sprigs of cilantro

For the chicken, pound the chicken between sheets of waxed paper or plastic wrap with a meat mallet until slightly flattened. Arrange the chicken in a single layer in a dish. Combine the brown sugar, vinegar, soy sauce, oil, orange zest, gingerroot, garlic and pepper in a bowl and mix well. Pour over the chicken, turning to coat. Marinate, covered, in the refrigerator for 4 hours, turning occasionally; drain. Grill or broil for 3 to 4 minutes or until the chicken is cooked through. Chill, covered, in the refrigerator. Cut the chicken into 3/4-inch pieces.

    For the salad, cook the wild rice using package directions. Chill in the refrigerator. Combine the chilled chicken, chilled rice, mangoes, carrots, cilantro and salt in a salad bowl. Drizzle with the Rice Wine Vinaigrette and gently toss. Garnish with sprigs of cilantro just before serving.

Serves 6

RICE WINE VINAIGRETTE

1/3 cup rice wine vinegar
3 tablespoons brewed black tea
1 tablespoon sugar

2 1/2 teaspoons Chinese chile paste
2 garlic cloves, finely minced
1/4 teaspoon pepper

Whisk all the ingredients in a bowl until the sugar dissolves. Chill.

Serves 6

MAESTRO JOHN WILLIAMS' SALAD

Maestro's salad, fresh white corn, and a glass of very nice California wine followed by two raisin brownies and a cup of hot tea will make a very happy picnic for Mr. Williams, according to Carmen Chiong, Mr. Williams' housekeeper.

2 tablespoons olive oil

2 tablespoons red wine vinegar

1 tablespoon Dijon mustard

1 tablespoon honey

1/4 teaspoon salt

1/4 teaspoon pepper

1 cup chopped barbecued chicken
   breast (below)

1 cup deveined peeled steamed shrimp

6 ounces garden rotini, cooked,
   drained

2 cups cherry tomatoes

1/2 cup cooked green peas

1/2 cup thinly sliced carrots

1/4 cup thinly sliced celery

Lettuce leaves

Whisk the olive oil, vinegar, Dijon mustard, honey, salt and pepper in a bowl until blended. Chill, covered, in the refrigerator. Combine the chicken, shrimp, pasta, cherry tomatoes, peas, carrots and celery in a salad bowl and mix well. Add the vinaigrette and toss to coat. Spoon the salad onto a lettuce-lined serving platter.

Serves 2

BARBECUED CHICKEN

2 boneless skinless chicken breasts

Juice of 1/2 lime

1 teaspoon chopped garlic

1/4 teaspoon salt

1/4 teaspoon pepper

Arrange the chicken in a dish. Whisk the lime juice, garlic, salt and pepper in a bowl. Drizzle over the chicken, turning to coat.

   Marinate, covered, in the refrigerator for 4 to 5 hours. Grill the chicken over hot coals until cooked through, turning occasionally. Cool slightly and cut into bite-size pieces.

Serves 2

PASTA SALAD WITH CHICKEN AND ARTICHOKES

16 ounces spiral pasta

1 (2 1/2- to 3-pound) chicken, cooked

2 (6-ounce) jars marinated artichoke
   hearts, drained

1 avocado, chopped

1 (5-ounce) jar green olives, drained,
   sliced

1 (3-ounce) jar capers, drained

4 green onions, chopped

Fresh Basil Dressing (below)

2 tomatoes, chopped

Cook the pasta using package directions; drain. Rinse in cold water and drain. Transfer the pasta to a large salad bowl. Shred the chicken, discarding the skin and bones.

Add the chicken, artichokes, avocado, olives, capers and green onions to the salad bowl and mix well. Drizzle with the Fresh Basil Dressing and mix well. Chill, covered, until serving time. Add the tomatoes and gently toss just before serving.

Serves 8

FRESH BASIL DRESSING

1 cup fresh basil leaves

2/3 cup olive oil

Juice of 1 lemon

1/4 cup red wine vinegar

1 tablespoon Dijon mustard

1 garlic clove, crushed

1/2 teaspoon cayenne pepper

Salt to taste

Combine the basil, olive oil, lemon juice, vinegar, Dijon mustard, garlic, cayenne pepper and salt in a blender or food processor container fitted with a steel blade. Process until smooth.

Serves 8

ROAST DUCK AND PEAR SALAD

Roast the duck early in the afternoon, and then skin and bone after cooling. The strong nutmeg infusion in the dressing pinches you awake at the first bite of lettuce. This recipe was taken from Michael Roberts' What's For Dinner, *(Wm. Morris & Co.).*

1 (5-pound) duck, dressed

1 cup chicken or duck stock or canned reduced-sodium chicken broth

1/8 teaspoon freshly grated nutmeg

1/2 cup malt vinegar

2 tablespoons honey

1/2 cup vegetable oil

1 firm ripe pear, peeled, cut into thin strips

1 small head red leaf lettuce, torn into bite-size pieces

Arrange the duck on a rack in a roasting pan. Roast at 425 degrees for 10 minutes. Reduce the oven temperature to 350 degrees. Roast for 1 1/2 hours longer. Drain the fat as it collects in the roasting pan during the roasting process, reserving 1 cup.

Remove the duck from the oven. Let stand until easily handled. Remove the skin and cut into 1/4-inch strips. Set aside. Remove all the meat from the bones. Cut the breast meat into 1/2×2-inch strips. Cut the thigh meat and leg meat into slivers approximately the same size. Set aside.

Heat the reserved fat in a heavy skillet to 325 degrees or until very hot. Fry the reserved duck skin in the hot fat for 3 minutes or until crisp; drain. Combine the stock and nutmeg in a small saucepan. Bring to a boil over high heat. Boil for 5 minutes or until reduced by half. Pour the stock mixture into a heatproof bowl. Stir in the vinegar and honey. Let stand until cool. Whisk in the oil until of a dressing consistency.

Add the pear to the dressing. Add the lettuce and toss to coat. Mound the lettuce mixture on 2 or 3 salad plates. Arrange the duck over the top. Sprinkle with the fried duck skin strips.

Wine Selection: Kendall-Jackson Vintner's Reserve Pinot Noir

Serves 2 to 3

JOACHIM SPLICHAL'S MAINE LOBSTER SALAD

1/2 teaspoon red wine vinegar

1/8 teaspoon sea salt

1 (1 1/2-pound) Maine lobster

1/2 cup fresh peas

1/2 cup fresh fava beans, shelled
(about 5 large pods)

3 small plum tomatoes, peeled,
seeded, chopped

1/4 cup (2 ounces) haricots verts

2 ribs celery, cut into 1/4-inch
julienne strips

1/4 cup (2 ounces) thin asparagus
spears, bottom 2 inches peeled

1/4 cup (2 ounces) baby carrots,
peeled with 1/4 inch of the green
top remaining

1/2 cup crème fraîche

2 tablespoons finely chopped fresh
chives

1 tablespoon lemon juice

1 teaspoon finely chopped lemon zest

1/2 cup oak leaf lettuce, arugula or
radicchio leaves

1 to 2 ounces (or more) Osetra caviar

Bring a generous amount of water to a boil in a stockpot. Add the vinegar and sea salt. Plunge the live lobster into the boiling water. Boil, covered, for 8 minutes; drain. Cool until easily handled. Remove the meat from the tail and claws. Slice the lobster meat into 1/2-inch-thick pieces. Set aside. If it will be more than 1 hour until serving time, chill the lobster meat.

Have ready a large bowl of ice water. Bring a generous amount of water to boil in a large saucepan. Blanch each of the vegetables separately in the boiling water for 4 minutes or until tender. Remove the vegetables with a skimmer and immediately plunge into the ice water. Let stand for 1 minute to stop the cooking process. Drain on a tea towel. Adjust the cooking time to the size and shape of the vegetables.

Combine the crème fraîche, chives, lemon juice and lemon zest in a bowl and whisk until blended. Combine the lobster and vegetables in a bowl and mix well. Add the dressing and gently toss until coated. Spoon 1/4 of the lobster mixture onto 4 lettuce-lined salad plates. Top with dollops of the caviar. Serve immediately.

Wine Selection: Kendall-Jackson Grand Reserve Sauvignon Blanc

Serves 4

SHRIMP SALAD WITH BALSAMIC VINAIGRETTE

This is a slightly simplified version of a beautiful salad recipe sent by Michael McCarty of Michael's Restaurant in Santa Monica. All of the ingredients are still here for your enjoyment.

4 medium tomatoes, peeled, seeded, cut into $1/4$-inch pieces

1 cup extra-virgin olive oil

$1/4$ cup sherry wine vinegar or other mild vinegar

2 tablespoons julienned fresh basil

$1/2$ shallot, finely chopped

Salt and pepper to taste

2 quarts mixed baby greens

3 medium ripe avocados, cut into halves, cut into $1/4$-inch slices

1 cup Maui Onion Confit (page 77)

18 medium shrimp, peeled, deveined (about 2 pounds)

3 tablespoons clarified butter

$1/4$ cup Balsamic Vinaigrette (page 77)

Combine the tomatoes, olive oil, vinegar, basil and shallot in a bowl and gently mix. Season with salt and pepper. Chill, covered, for 30 minutes or longer.

Arrange the salad greens on 6 plates or 1 large serving platter. Arrange the avocado slices around the edge of the greens. Spoon some of the Maui Onion Confit in the center of each of the plates. Surround the Onion Confit with the tomato mixture.

Brush the shrimp with the clarified butter. Grill or broil for 1 minute per side or until the shrimp turn pink, rotating the shrimp 90 degrees while cooking to give them a crisscross pattern. Arrange 3 shrimp on each plate or around the edge of the platter. Drizzle with the Balsamic Vinaigrette.

Serves 6

MAUI ONION CONFIT

1 medium Maui, Vidalia or Walla Walla onion, thinly sliced
2 tablespoons water
1 cup (2 sticks) butter, cut into 1-inch pieces
Salt and white pepper to taste
Fresh lemon juice to taste

Combine the onion, water and 1 piece of the butter in a small heavy saucepan. Cook, covered, over low heat until tender, stirring occasionally; drain. Add the remaining butter gradually, stirring with a wooden spoon until the butter is melted and absorbed by the onions. Season with salt, white pepper and lemon juice.

Makes 1 cup

BALSAMIC VINAIGRETTE

2/3 cup extra-virgin olive oil
1/3 cup balsamic vinegar
Fresh lime juice to taste
Salt and freshly ground white pepper to taste

Whisk the olive oil and balsamic vinegar in a bowl until blended. Season with lime juice, salt and white pepper.

Makes 1 cup

1937 *Composer and conductor Ferde Grofé conducted his ballet* Grand Canyon *before an audience of 21,000, the highest for a single night of ballet. Grofé had joined the Los Angeles Philharmonic as a violist in 1919, in its very first season.*

KATE MANTILINI'S SHRIMP COBB SALAD

Favorite salad of pianist Yefim Bronfman.

4 cups wild organic greens
$1/4$ to $1/2$ cup favorite vinaigrette
Lime juice
1 avocado, chopped
1 cup finely chopped or grated hard-cooked eggs or egg whites
1 cup crumbled crisp-cooked bacon
1 cup crumbled feta cheese or Danish bleu cheese
1 cup coarsely chopped cooked fresh shrimp
Sprigs of watercress
Niçoise olives

Toss the greens with $1/4$ cup of the vinaigrette in a bowl. Line 4 plates evenly with the greens. Drizzle lime juice over the avocado in a bowl and gently toss to coat. Arrange $1/4$ of the avocado, $1/4$ of the eggs, $1/4$ of the bacon, $1/4$ of the feta cheese and $1/4$ of the shrimp in rows over the greens on each plate. Drizzle with desired amount of remaining vinaigrette. Top with sprigs of watercress. Pass olives with the salad.

Serves 4

1938   *For truly "grand" opera, nothing is likely to surpass the Bowl's production of Die Walkure, starring Maria Jeritza as Brunhilde: dazzling lighting effects, genuine fire and smoke, and, in the famous "ride," Valkyries on white horses careening down the hillsides onto the stage.*

BABY POTATO SALAD WITH SEARED TUNA

From Joachim Splichal at Café Pinot, the salad that almost defines a picnic becomes a very special entrée.

1 pound tuna, cut into 1/2-inch cubes

1 tablespoon extra-virgin olive oil

1/4 ounce freshly ground pepper

1 pound baby potatoes, such as fingerling, red or white new potatoes

1/2 bunch scallions, thinly sliced

1/4 bunch radishes, thinly sliced

1/2 red onion, grilled, chopped

1 teaspoon (or more) prepared horseradish

2 teaspoons Champagne vinegar

2 tablespoons grapeseed oil or light vegetable oil

Lettuce leaves

Fresh chives

Brush the tuna with the olive oil and sprinkle with the pepper. Combine the potatoes with enough cold water to cover in a saucepan. Cook until tender; drain. Let stand until cool. Cut the potatoes into quarters. Combine the potatoes, scallions, radishes and onion in a bowl and mix well.

Whisk the horseradish, vinegar and grapeseed oil in a bowl until blended. Add the horseradish mixture to the potato mixture and toss to mix. Spoon the potato mixture onto a lettuce-lined platter.

Sear the tuna in a hot nonstick sauté pan until rare or medium-rare. Remove from heat. Let stand until cool. Arrange the tuna over the potato salad. Garnish with fresh chives.

Serves 4

SEAFOOD AND PEARL PASTA SALAD

This recipe hails from Lunaria Restaurant and Jazz Club owner, Bernard Jacoupy.

1 cup pearl pasta	1/2 cup sliced wood ear mushrooms
1/2 cup white wine	1/2 cup mayonnaise
24 mussels	4 garlic cloves, chopped
1 pinch of saffron	1/2 cup frozen peas
12 shrimp, peeled, deveined	1 red bell pepper, chopped
32 bay scallops	Salt and freshly ground pepper
4 squid, cleaned, sliced	to taste

Cook the pasta in boiling water in a saucepan until tender; drain. Let stand until cool. Bring the wine to a boil in a large saucepan. Add the mussels. Cook, covered, for 4 minutes or until the mussels open. Drain, reserving the liquid. Remove the mussels from the shells and set aside.

Combine the saffron with the reserved liquid. Cook until reduced to 1/4 cup. Let stand until cool. Steam the shrimp, scallops, squid and mushrooms for 3 minutes; drain.

Combine the mayonnaise with the saffron reduction in a bowl and mix well. Stir in the garlic. Combine the pasta, mussels, shrimp, scallops, squid, mushrooms, peas and bell pepper in a bowl and mix well. Add the mayonnaise mixture and toss to coat. Season with salt and pepper.

Serves 4 to 6

1939   *In September, Benny Goodman, the most famous clarinetist of his time, followed his previous year's performance at Carnegie Hall with a stint at the Bowl. The response was varied—the "long hairs" versus the "hep cats"—with many disruptive outbursts from the audience. It wasn't until the late 1950s that jazz became a regular part of every summer's season.*

25^c

Hollywood Bowl

1st week
July 6, 8, 9, 10, 11, 1965

ENTREES

FILET OF BEEF IN PHYLLO

Accompany with a horseradish and sour cream sauce, garnished with chopped chives.

1 (3-pound) filet mignon, trimmed
Salt to taste
2 tablespoons unsalted butter
8 ounces mushrooms, minced
2 shallots, minced
1 (16-ounce) package phyllo pastry, thawed
1/2 cup (1 stick or more) butter, melted

Rub the filet with salt. Heat 2 tablespoons unsalted butter in a heavy skillet over high heat. Sear the filet in the butter for 45 minutes or until rare and brown on all sides. Remove the filet to a platter, reserving the pan juices. Cool slightly. Chill in the refrigerator for 1 hour or longer.

Sauté the mushrooms and shallots in the reserved pan juices for 2 to 3 minutes or until tender. Layer 12 sheets of the pastry brushing each layer with some of the melted butter. (While working with the pastry, keep it covered with a damp tea towel or it will dry out and become impossible to work with.) Spread half the mushroom mixture on the pastry and place the chilled filet on top. Spread the remaining mushroom mixture over the top of the filet and fold the pastry around the filet.

Brush an additional 5 or 6 sheets of the pastry with melted butter. Seal all the edges by overlapping them with the additional pastry and brush with melted butter. Arrange the pastry-wrapped filet in a buttered baking pan. Bake at 400 degrees for 45 to 50 minutes or until the pastry is brown and flaky. Chill, covered, in the refrigerator. Slice as desired with a very sharp knife.

Wine Selection: Kendall-Jackson Grand Reserve Merlot

Serves 10 to 12

TOP SIRLOIN STEAK

1 top sirloin steak, 1 1/2 to 2 inches thick
Cucumber curls, sprigs of watercress and/or parsley
French Mustard Sauce (page 85)
Sour Cream Dill Sauce (page 85)

Arrange the steak on a rack in a broiler pan. Broil until a meat thermometer registers 140 degrees. Wrap the steak in a double thickness of heavy-duty foil immediately. Freeze for about 1 hour. Transfer the steak to the refrigerator; do not unwrap. Store in the refrigerator until serving time.

Just before serving, unwrap the steak and reserve the juices. Slice across the grain into the desired thickness. Arrange the sliced steak on a serving platter and drizzle with the reserved juices. Garnish with cucumber curls, sprigs of watercress and/or sprigs of parsley. Serve with French Mustard Sauce and/or Sour Cream Dill Sauce.

Wine Selection: Kendall-Jackson Vintner's Reserve Cabernet Sauvignon

Serves 1 or 2

1940 *The entrance of the Hollywood Bowl is graced by a serene fountain topped by a 15-foot statue of the Muse of Music and smaller figures of the Muses of Dance and Drama. It was designed by George Stanley, creator of the Oscar statuette, and erected through a collaborative effort of the County of Los Angeles Engineer's Department, the WPA, and the Southern California Arts Project.*

FRENCH MUSTARD SAUCE

3 tablespoons dry mustard
1 tablespoon sugar
1 teaspoon cornstarch
1 egg, lightly beaten
3/4 cup mild vinegar
Olive oil

Combine the dry mustard, sugar and cornstarch in a saucepan and mix well. Stir in the egg. Add the vinegar and mix well. Cook over low to medium heat until slightly thickened, stirring constantly. Remove from heat. Let stand until cool. Add enough olive oil until the sauce is of the desired consistency and mix well.

You may store the sauce, covered, in the refrigerator for several weeks. Decrease the amount of dry mustard for a milder flavor. Use the vinegar from a jar of sweet pickles, malt vinegar or a mild vinegar with pineapple juice added for the mild vinegar.

Makes 1 cup

SOUR CREAM DILL SAUCE

1 cup sour cream
1 tablespoon white wine vinegar
1 teaspoon dillweed
1 teaspoon celery salt
1/2 teaspoon sugar

Combine the sour cream, vinegar, dillweed, celery salt and sugar in a bowl and mix well. Store, covered, in the refrigerator.

Makes 1 cup

PARSI BEEF CUTLETS

According to Tehmi Mehta, this makes a good side dish, or serve as a sandwich between two slices of your favorite bread for picnics.

3 slices white bread, or 4 ounces
   mashed potatoes

18 ounces ground beef

6 garlic cloves

1 (1-inch) piece fresh gingerroot

2 medium onions, finely chopped

2 to 4 green chiles, finely chopped

8 fresh mint leaves

2 tablespoons finely chopped cilantro

2 dessert spoons Worcestershire sauce

1 teaspoon salt

3/4 teaspoon turmeric

3/4 cup dry unseasoned bread
   crumbs

2 egg whites

2 egg yolks

Salt to taste

Vegetable oil for frying

Combine the bread with enough water to cover in a bowl. Soak for 10 minutes. Squeeze the excess moisture from the bread. Add the bread to the ground beef in a bowl and mix well. Grind the garlic and gingerroot until of a paste consistency. Add the garlic mixture, onions, green chiles, mint, cilantro, Worcestershire sauce, 1 teaspoon salt and turmeric to the ground beef mixture and mix well. Chill, covered, for 1 hour.

Divide the ground beef mixture into 12 equal portions and shape each portion into a cutlet. Coat both sides of each cutlet with bread crumbs. Beat the egg whites in a bowl until frothy. Add the egg yolks. Beat until blended. Stir in salt to taste.

Add enough oil to a large skillet to measure 1/2 inch. Heat over medium heat. Dip each cutlet in the eggs and fry in the hot oil until brown on both sides; drain. You may substitute 1 teaspoon garlic powder for the garlic cloves and 1 teaspoon ground ginger for the gingerroot.

Makes 12 cutlets

PICADILLO

A picnic favorite of Marilyn Horne, who finds that although the recipe calls for it to be served hot, it is just as good served cold or at room temperature. Also, it works well substituting ground turkey for half the beef.

1/3 cup dried currants

1 tablespoon peanut, vegetable, corn
   or olive oil

1 cup finely chopped onion

1 tablespoon finely chopped garlic

1 cup chopped green bell pepper

3 to 4 ounces stuffed green olives

1 (3-ounce) jar capers, drained

2 1/2 tablespoons white vinegar

1 teaspoon freshly ground pepper

1/3 teaspoon ground cloves

1/4 teaspoon cinnamon

1 bay leaf

Tabasco sauce to taste

Salt to taste

1 tablespoon peanut, vegetable, corn
   or olive oil

2 pounds ground round or ground
   chuck

4 cups chopped peeled tomatoes

Hot cooked rice

Plump the currants in a bowl in enough warm water to cover for 30 minutes; drain. Heat 1 tablespoon peanut oil in a skillet. Stir in the onion, garlic and bell pepper. Cook until tender, stirring constantly. Stir in the olives, capers, vinegar, pepper, cloves, cinnamon, bay leaf, Tabasco sauce and salt. Cook for 10 minutes, stirring frequently.

Heat 1 tablespoon peanut oil in a Dutch oven. Add the ground round. Cook until the beef loses its red color, stirring to break up the lumps; drain. Stir in the olive mixture and currants. Add the tomatoes and mix well. Cook for 1 hour, stirring frequently and skimming off the fat as needed. Discard the bay leaf. Spoon over hot cooked rice.

Serves 6

HOLLYWOOD BOWL ORIGINAL CHICKEN-IN-A-BASKET

A wonderful picnic dinner before a concert.

1 large round loaf French bread	Flour
Butter, softened	Salt and pepper
Rosemary, basil and oregano to taste	Vegetable oil
1 (2^1/2- to 3-pound) chicken, cut up	

Cut the top from the bread loaf to make a basket, reserving the top. Remove the center carefully, leaving a ^{1}/2-inch shell. Coat the inside of the basket with butter. Sprinkle with rosemary, basil and oregano or your favorite herbs.

Coat the chicken with a mixture of the flour, salt and pepper. Fry the chicken in a mixture of butter and oil in a skillet until brown on all sides; drain. Place the chicken in the bread basket and replace the top. Wrap in foil.

Bake at 300 degrees for 1 hour. Remove the basket from the oven and wrap in newspapers for transportation to a picnic. Unwrap the loaf and enjoy both the chicken and bread. Serve with a salad and wine.

Serves 6

1941 *Notoriously demanding about perfect conditions, Vladimir Horowitz discovered that he "sounded good" at the Bowl. For his debut, he played Rachmaninoff's Concerto No. 2. Later, with his friend Rachmaninoff in the audience, Horowitz played the Concerto No. 3. At the conclusion of the concert, Rachmaninoff walked on stage, took Horowitz by the hand, and told the pianist, "This is how I had always dreamed the concerto should be played."*

SPICY CHICKEN-IN-A-BASKET

1 (8-inch) round loaf sourdough bread

1/4 cup (1/2 stick) butter, softened

2 tablespoons chopped Italian parsley

4 teaspoons Italian herbs

1 teaspoon garlic powder

4 boneless skinless chicken breasts

Salt to taste

1/2 cup flour

1 tablespoon paprika

1/4 teaspoon pepper

Cut the top from the bread loaf to make a basket, reserving the top. Remove the center carefully, leaving a 1/2-inch shell. Combine the butter, parsley, Italian herbs and garlic powder in a bowl and mix well. Brush the butter mixture over the inside of the bread basket.

Sprinkle the chicken with salt. Coat with a mixture of the flour, paprika and pepper. Sauté the chicken in a skillet for 7 minutes on each side or until brown. Place the chicken in the bread basket and replace the top. Wrap in foil. Bake at 350 degrees for 30 to 40 minutes. Wrap with newspapers to transport to a picnic. Serve each guest a piece of the chicken and a piece of the basket.

Serves 4

PERFECT CHICKEN PICNIC-IN-A-BASKET

This is another variation using the dark meat of the chicken.

$1/2$ cup flour

$1^1/2$ tablespoons sesame seeds

$2^1/4$ teaspoons tarragon

$1^1/2$ teaspoons thyme

$1^1/2$ teaspoons poppy seeds

1 teaspoon salt

1 teaspoon pepper

4 chicken thighs

4 chicken legs

2 egg whites, lightly beaten

2 tablespoons butter

2 tablespoons margarine

1 round loaf sourdough bread

Buttery Herb Sauce (below)

Combine the flour, sesame seeds, tarragon, thyme, poppy seeds, salt and pepper in a shallow dish and mix well. Dip the chicken in the egg whites and coat with the flour mixture. Heat the butter and margarine in a 10- to 12-inch skillet over medium heat. Brown the chicken in the butter mixture for 7 minutes per side; drain. Arrange the chicken in a 3-quart baking dish. Bake, covered, at 350 degrees for 30 minutes; remove the cover. Bake for 10 minutes longer to crisp the chicken.

Cut the top from the bread loaf to make a basket, reserving the top. Remove the center carefully, leaving a $3/4$-inch shell. Brush the inside of the basket with the Buttery Herb Sauce. Place the basket and reserved top on a baking sheet. Arrange the chicken in the basket. Bake, uncovered, for 20 minutes. Replace the top and wrap the basket in several layers of foil and then newspaper. The basket will remain warm for several hours. Serve each guest 2 pieces of chicken and a piece of the basket.

Serves 4

BUTTERY HERB SAUCE

$1/4$ cup ($1/2$ stick) butter

3 tablespoons sesame seeds

1 tablespoon thyme

1 tablespoon tarragon

1 tablespoon poppy seeds

Heat the butter in a saucepan until melted. Stir in the remaining ingredients.

Makes $1/3$ cup

MOROCCAN CHICKEN

Serve with Armenian flat bread and Tabbouleh (page 61).

1/3 cup olive oil

1 large onion, sliced

1 large garlic clove, chopped

2 tablespoons (heaping) chopped cilantro

2 tablespoons (heaping) chopped parsley

1 (2 1/2- to 3-pound) chicken, cut up, skinned

1 small lemon, sliced

1/2 teaspoon salt

1/2 teaspoon pepper

1/8 teaspoon saffron

1/2 cup small green olives with pits

Heat the olive oil in a large skillet over medium heat. Sauté the onion and garlic in the hot olive oil for 5 to 10 minutes or until the onion is tender. Stir in the cilantro and parsley. Add the chicken.

Sauté for 2 minutes on each side. Place a lemon slice on top of each chicken piece. Sprinkle with the salt, pepper and saffron. Cook, covered, over low heat for 1 hour, stirring occasionally. Stir in the olives. Cook for 30 minutes longer, stirring occasionally.

Serves 4 to 5

1943 *Study in contrasts: On August 8, Bruno Walter conducted his final Bowl concert and said an emotional farewell to Southern California. At intermission, an announcement was made that a sensational singer named Frank Sinatra had been engaged for a Bowl appearance. When "Frankie" did appear, screaming females (and not all teenagers!) quickly exceeded the audience limitation of 10,000, despite the efforts of police and Bowl personnel. The Bowl ended in the black that year, thanks to this overwhelming response to Sinatra's performance.*

FIVE-SPICE CORNISH GAME HENS

4 Cornish game hens
1/4 cup sesame oil
4 teaspoons five-spice powder
4 teaspoons grated orange zest
1 teaspoon cayenne pepper
4 (quarter-size) pieces gingerroot
8 green onion bulbs
1/4 cup honey, heated

Brush the hens with the sesame oil. Mix the five-spice powder, orange zest and cayenne pepper in a bowl. Sprinkle the spice mixture over the hens. Place 1 piece of the gingerroot and 2 green onion bulbs in each hen cavity.

Arrange the hens on a rack in a roasting pan. Drizzle with the warm honey. Bake at 350 degrees for 1 hour or until golden brown and cooked through, basting occasionally with the pan juices.

Wine Selection: Kendall-Jackson Vintner's Reserve Chardonnay

Serves 4

1945 *Leopold Stokowski, Music Director of the Bowl in 1945 and 1946, endeared himself to members of the orchestra when he insisted that a covering be set up during rehearsals to shield the players and their instruments from the harsh sun. Prior to that, only the conductor had enjoyed the shade of a large beach umbrella spread over the podium. Stokowski also revived the custom of Community Sing and always complimented the audience on its participation.*

BOBOTIE

This South African recipe won the Grand Prize for the team of Ernest Fleischmann and Lyn Kienholz in the 1986 March of Dimes Celebrity Cook-Off.

2 (1-inch-thick) slices white bread,
    cubed
2 cups milk
1 1/2 pounds ground lamb or beef
1 1/2 medium onions, coarsely
    chopped
2 garlic cloves, crushed
2 tablespoons vegetable oil
1 1/2 tablespoons (or less) curry
    powder
1 tablespoon turmeric
1 teaspoon ginger
1 teaspoon salt

1 teaspoon pepper
1 large tomato, peeled, finely
    chopped
1 large tart green cooking apple,
    chopped
1/3 cup seedless raisins
1/4 cup almonds, blanched, chopped
    (optional)
3 tablespoons mango chutney
1 tablespoon lemon juice
1 tablespoon Worcestershire sauce
1 tablespoon apricot jam
4 eggs

Soak the bread in the milk in a bowl. Cook the ground lamb in a skillet just until most of the juices have been released, stirring frequently; drain. Cook the onions and garlic in the oil in a skillet over low heat until tender, stirring frequently. Stir in the curry powder, turmeric, ginger, salt and pepper. Simmer for 2 minutes, stirring occasionally. A small amount of water may be added if the mixture is too thick.

Combine the lamb, onion mixture, tomato, apple, raisins, almonds, chutney, lemon juice, Worcestershire sauce and jam in a bowl and mix well. Squeeze the milk from the bread, reserving the milk. Add the bread to the lamb mixture and mix well. Pat the lamb mixture to within 1 1/2 inches of the top edge of a large baking dish.

Whisk the reserved milk and eggs in a bowl until blended. Add enough additional milk to measure 2 cups. Pour the milk mixture over the top of the ground lamb mixture. Bake at 350 degrees for 1 hour or until the top layer is light brown and set. Serve with boiled rice and various condiments such as chopped bananas, sliced scallions, shredded coconut, chutney or peanuts.

Serves 4 to 6

CURRIED LAMB PATTY

Your taste buds will be happily surprised at this quick and easy recipe with a Middle Eastern flavor.

1 pound ground lamb
1/2 cup wheat germ
1/2 cup milk
1 egg, lightly beaten
1 tablespoon dried minced onion
1 tablespoon curry powder
1 tablespoon lemon juice
1 tablespoon chopped chutney
1/2 teaspoon salt
1/4 cup sliced almonds

Combine the ground lamb, wheat germ, milk, egg, minced onion, curry powder, lemon juice, chutney and salt in a bowl and mix well. Pat the ground lamb mixture into a 9-inch round baking dish. Sprinkle with the almonds.

Bake at 350 degrees for 45 minutes or until brown and cooked through. Cut into wedges. Serve hot or cold.

Wine Selection: Kendall-Jackson Vintner's Reserve Merlot

Serves 4

STUFFED PRETTY PICNIC PORK

This is a do-ahead dish that is beautiful to behold.

1 (7-inch) center-cut pork loin roast

Salt to taste

4 ounces pitted prunes

4 ounces dried apricots

2 tablespoons olive oil or peanut oil

1 large carrot, thinly sliced

1 medium onion, thinly sliced

2 ribs celery, thinly sliced

3 garlic cloves

1 cup chicken stock

1 cup sweet vermouth, marsala or
   port

$1/2$ teaspoon thyme

Pepper to taste

$1/2$ to 1 teaspoon arrowroot

Have the butcher trim the fat and bone the roast. Cut a slit lengthwise through the loin, being careful not to cut through the walls. Rub the cavity of the roast with salt. Insert prunes and apricots alternately until the cavity is full and the roast takes on a cylindrical shape. Secure the ends with crossed wooden picks.

Heat the olive oil in a Dutch oven. Blot the moisture from the roast with paper towels. Brown the roast on all sides in the hot oil for about 10 minutes, turning frequently. Remove the roast to a platter, reserving the pan drippings.

Add the carrot, onion, celery and garlic to the reserved pan drippings. Sauté until light brown. Tilt the pan and blot any extra pan drippings with a paper towel. Stir in the stock, wine and thyme. Return the roast to the pan and sprinkle with salt and pepper. Bring to a boil.

Bake, covered, at 350 degrees for 45 minutes; do not overcook. Remove the roast to a platter. Let stand until cool. Force the pan drippings and vegetables through a sieve into a saucepan. Cool slightly and skim the fat. Bring to a boil. Boil until reduced by half, stirring frequently. Taste and adjust seasonings.

Mix the arrowroot in a small amount of cold water in a bowl. Stir the arrowroot mixture into the pan dripping mixture. Cook until slightly thickened and of a sauce consistency, stirring frequently. Let stand until cool. Chill, covered, for 8 to 10 hours. Wrap the roast tightly in foil and chill for 8 to 10 hours. To serve, slice the roast into $1/2$-inch slices with a sharp knife and serve over the chilled sauce.

Wine Selection: Kendall-Jackson Vintner's Reserve Pinot Noir

Serves 4 to 6

ANGEL ROMERO'S SHELLFISH STEW
CAZUELA DE MARISCOS DE ANGEL ROMERO

Angel Romero's Shellfish Stew is as finely tuned as his guitar.

1/2 cup extra-virgin olive oil

1 bulb garlic, separated into cloves,
  minced

2 cups chopped white onions

5 tomatoes

2 bay leaves

1 tablespoon oregano

2 teaspoons salt

1/8 teaspoon pepper

1 pinch of saffron

1 (6-ounce) can tomato paste

1 cup clam juice

1/2 cup dry white wine

15 mussels, cleaned

15 clams, cleaned

15 prawns, shelled

1 pound firm white fish, cut into large
  chunks

Heat the olive oil in a large sauté pan. Add the garlic. Sauté for 1 minute. Stir in the onions. Sauté for 8 to 10 minutes or until the onions are tender. Stir in the tomatoes, bay leaves, oregano, salt, pepper and saffron.

Simmer for 10 minutes or until the tomatoes are tender, stirring frequently. Stir in the tomato paste, clam juice and wine. Simmer for 15 minutes or until thickened, stirring occasionally.

Place the mussels, clams, prawns and white fish in a large ovenproof pan. Spoon the tomato sauce over the seafood. Bake at 350 degrees until the clams and mussels open. Discard the bay leaves. Remove the seafood to a large bowl or 6 serving bowls with a slotted spoon. Stir the sauce and pour over the seafood. Serve immediately with crusty sourdough bread.

Serves 6

1947 *On August 20, Margaret Truman, the only child of President Harry S Truman, starred in a Bowl performance. She was well received by the 11,100 people in the audience. The critics were less kind.*

POACHED SALMON WITH WATERCRESS CREAM SAUCE

Butter, softened

2 shallots, minced

4 salmon steaks, $1/2$ to $3/4$ inch thick

1 cup dry white wine

$1/3$ cup bottled clam juice

1 cup sour cream

$1/4$ cup minced fresh watercress leaves

2 tablespoons fresh lime juice

1 tablespoon Pommery mustard

Salt and pepper to taste

Coat the bottom and side of a stainless steel or enameled skillet large enough to hold the salmon in a single layer with butter. Sprinkle the shallots over the bottom. Arrange the salmon over the shallots. Pour the wine and clam juice over the top. Bring to a boil over medium heat; reduce the heat.

Simmer, covered, for 20 minutes or just until the salmon flakes when tested with a fork. Remove the salmon to a platter with a slotted spoon, reserving the pan juices; discard the skin. Chill, covered, for 1 hour.

Bring the reserved pan juices to a boil over high heat. Cook until the juices are reduced to about $1/4$ cup. Remove from heat. Let stand until cool. Add the sour cream, watercress, lime juice and Pommery mustard to the reduction and stir until of a sauce consistency. Season with salt and pepper. Chill, covered, until serving time. Serve the watercress sauce with the salmon.

Serves 4

WOLFGANG PUCK'S COLD SEA BASS PROVENCAL

6 anchovy fillets

Milk

1/4 cup olive oil

1 cup finely chopped onion

8 garlic cloves, finely chopped

2 tablespoons finely chopped
  fresh thyme

1 teaspoon chile flakes

4 cups chopped seeded peeled
  tomatoes

1 pinch of saffron (optional)

3 tablespoons finely chopped
  niçoise olives

3 tablespoons finely chopped
  fresh basil

Salt and pepper to taste

2 1/2 pounds sea bass, skinned,
  boned, cut into 6 equal portions

1 tablespoon finely chopped
  fresh thyme

1/4 cup olive oil

White wine

Soak the anchovy fillets with enough milk to cover in a bowl for 5 to 10 minutes; drain. Heat a heavy saucepan over high heat. Add 1/4 cup olive oil. Sauté the onion, garlic, 2 tablespoons thyme and chile flakes in the hot olive oil until the onion is tender. Stir in the anchovy fillets.

Cook for 1 to 2 minutes, stirring frequently. Stir in the tomatoes and saffron. Cook for 10 minutes, stirring occasionally. Remove from heat. Stir in the olives and basil. Season with salt and pepper.

Sprinkle the fish with 1 tablespoon thyme, salt and pepper. Drizzle with 1/4 cup olive oil. Brown the fish on both sides in a baking pan or gratin dish. Deglaze with wine. Bring to a boil. Spoon the tomato mixture over the fish. Bake at 400 degrees for 10 to 15 minutes or until the fish flakes easily. Remove from oven. Let stand until cool. Chill, covered, in the refrigerator.

Arrange the fish on a decorative platter just before serving. Drizzle with additional olive oil and sprinkle with additional fresh basil and black olives. You may prepare up to 1 day in advance and store, covered, in the refrigerator.

Wine Selection: Kendall-Jackson Reserve Pinot Noir

Serves 6

Performing Arts

LOS ANGELES PHILHARMONIC

CARLO MARIA GIULINI
MUSIC DIRECTOR

HOLLYWOOD BOWL
summer festival
1979

JULY 4-7

50¢

Side Dishes and Quiches

ASPARAGUS WITH LEMON VINAIGRETTE

Substitute canned or homemade Hollandaise sauce for the Lemon Vinaigrette for variety.

Zest of 1 lemon, cut into very thin strips

Salt to taste

2 pounds asparagus spears, trimmed

1/3 cup fresh lemon juice

2 tablespoons finely chopped fresh rosemary

2 garlic cloves, minced

1 cup olive oil

Pepper to taste

Cook the lemon zest in boiling salted water in a large saucepan for 3 minutes. Remove the zest with a slotted spoon to a bowl. Return the water to a boil. Add the asparagus. Cook for 4 minutes or until tender-crisp; drain. Rinse under cold water; drain. Let stand until cool. Arrange the asparagus on individual plates.

Whisk the lemon juice, rosemary and garlic in a small bowl. Add the olive oil gradually, whisking constantly. Season with salt and pepper. Spoon the vinaigrette over the asparagus. Top each serving with some of the lemon zest.

Serves 6

1951 *Dorothy Buffum Chandler—in the space of 12 days—saved a financially troubled Hollywood Bowl and galvanized it into a successful new life. On Saturday, July 15, newspapers carried the shocking story that the Hollywood Bowl had closed. Contributions were decreasing, and an extravagant and ill-advised production of* Die Fledermaus *tipped the scales. "Buff," as she was known, wife of Norman Chandler, publisher of the Los Angeles Times, had been recently elected to the Bowl Board of Directors. She was made chairman of an emergency committee and spearheaded a campaign, the Crusade for Survival, to raise $100,000. Contributions of talent by well-known conductors and soloists, and pro bono support of the orchestra, helped the Bowl survive the crisis.*

MARINATED ARTICHOKE HEARTS AND MUSHROOMS

1 cup olive oil

1/2 cup red wine vinegar

2 teaspoons sugar

3 garlic cloves, minced

1 pound whole mushrooms

1 large can pitted green olives, drained

2 (8-ounce) cans artichoke hearts, drained

1 Bermuda onion, chopped

1/3 cup chopped pimentos

1/2 bunch parsley, trimmed, chopped

Whisk the olive oil, vinegar, sugar and garlic in a large bowl. Add the mushrooms, olives, artichokes, onion, pimentos and parsley and gently toss. Marinate, covered, in the refrigerator for 1 to 2 days, stirring occasionally.

Serves 6 to 8

GREEN BEAN BUNDLES

Fresh whole green beans

Thyme to taste

Salt to taste

Pimento strips or red bell pepper strips

Cook the beans and thyme in boiling salted water in a saucepan for 3 minutes or until al dente; drain. Arrange the green beans in bundles and tie with pimento or bell pepper strips in an X shape.

Variable servings

MAKE-AHEAD MARINATED WHITE BEANS

¹/3 cup lemon juice

¹/3 cup olive oil

Salt and pepper to taste

2 (15-ounce) cans Great Northern beans, drained, rinsed

1 large tomato, chopped

2 green onions, chopped

2 hard-cooked eggs, sliced

Whisk the lemon juice, olive oil, salt and pepper in a bowl. Add the beans and mix to coat. Marinate, covered, in the refrigerator for 24 hours, stirring occasionally. Stir in the tomato and green onions just before serving. Taste and add additional salt if needed. Garnish with sliced eggs.

Serves 4 to 6

1952   *After years of being forbidden the pleasure of bringing food into the seating area of the Bowl, music lovers were finally invited (even encouraged) to bring in their picnic baskets, delicacies, and spirits for before-the-performance enjoyment. Prizes were even offered for the most elegant and the most amusing dinner displays.*

BROCCOLI WITH PEANUT VINAIGRETTE

A good choice for a picnic, according to former Supervisor Edmund D. Edelman, one of the Bowl's most dedicated supporters and a cultural treasure of the city.

4^1/2 cups broccoli florets

Salt to taste

^{1}/2 cup roasted unsalted peanuts

^{1}/2 cup water

^{1}/2 cup olive oil

^{1}/4 cup red wine vinegar

^{1}/2 teaspoon salt

^{1}/8 teaspoon freshly ground pepper

Blanch the broccoli in boiling salted water in a medium saucepan for 3 minutes; drain. Plunge the broccoli into a bowl of ice water immediately to stop the cooking process; drain.

Process the peanuts in a blender or food processor until finely ground. Whisk the peanuts, water, olive oil, vinegar, ^{1}/2 teaspoon salt and pepper in a bowl until a vinaigrette forms. Add the broccoli and gently toss to coat. Serve immediately or store, covered, in the refrigerator for up to 8 hours.

Serves 6

1953 *Peggy Lee made her debut and soon became one of the Bowl's favorite vocalists. She returned many times, most recently in 1995.*

PICKLED BRUSSELS SPROUTS

8 ounces brussels sprouts

6 tablespoons vegetable oil

2 tablespoons red wine vinegar

1 tablespoon finely chopped onion

1 tablespoon chopped fresh parsley

1 small garlic clove, minced

1 1/2 teaspoons Dijon mustard

3/4 teaspoon dillweed

Combine the brussels sprouts with enough water to cover in a saucepan. Bring to a boil. Boil just until tender; drain.

Whisk the oil, vinegar, onion, parsley, garlic, Dijon mustard and dillweed in a bowl until mixed. Add the brussels sprouts and gently toss to coat. Chill, covered, for 8 to 10 hours; drain. You may store the brussels sprouts in the refrigerator for 2 to 3 days.

Serves 2 to 3

RED CABBAGE

A beautiful burgundy-colored side dish.

1 medium head red cabbage,
   shredded

2 medium apples, finely chopped

1/2 cup vinegar

1/2 cup water

1/2 cup packed brown sugar

2 tablespoons vegetable oil

1 teaspoon salt

1/2 teaspoon caraway seeds

1/4 teaspoon pepper

Combine the cabbage, apples, vinegar, water, brown sugar, oil, salt, caraway seeds and pepper in a large bowl and mix well. Transfer the cabbage mixture to a large skillet. Bring to a boil; reduce the heat.

Simmer for 1 hour or just until the cabbage is tender, stirring occasionally.

Serves 6

MARINATED CARROTS

2 pounds carrots, peeled, sliced
1 medium onion, thinly sliced,
    separated into rings
1 medium green bell pepper,
    thinly sliced
1 (10-ounce) can tomato soup

1 cup sugar
3/4 cup vinegar
1/2 cup vegetable oil
1 teaspoon salt
1 teaspoon pepper

Combine the carrots with enough water to cover in a saucepan. Cook for 20 minutes or until tender-crisp; drain. Let stand until cool. Combine the carrots, onion and bell pepper in a bowl and mix well.

Combine the soup, sugar, vinegar, oil, salt and pepper in a saucepan and mix well. Bring to a boil. Boil until the sugar dissolves, stirring frequently. Pour the hot soup mixture over the carrot mixture and stir to mix. Let stand until cool. Chill, covered, for 8 to 10 hours. Serve cold.

Serves 8 to 10

EGGPLANT SANDWICHES

1 cup bread crumbs
1/2 cup grated Parmesan cheese
1/3 cup chopped fresh parsley
Sliced mozzarella or provolone
    cheese

1 large eggplant, cut into
    1/2-inch slices
2 eggs, beaten
Vegetable oil

Mix the bread crumbs, Parmesan cheese and parsley in a shallow dish. Arrange 1 slice of mozzarella cheese on half the eggplant slices. Top with the remaining eggplant slices to form a sandwich.

Dip the sandwiches in the eggs and coat with the bread crumb mixture. Arrange the sandwiches in a single layer in a baking dish. Drizzle both sides of the sandwiches with oil. Bake at 375 degrees for 40 minutes or until the eggplant is tender, turning once. Serve hot or cold.

Serves 4 to 6

MARINATED TOMATOES

Chopped tomatoes

Chopped red onion

Cubed Monterey Jack or mozzarella
   cheese

Minced or crushed garlic

Crushed oregano to taste

Salt and pepper to taste

Olive oil to taste

Combine the tomatoes, onion, cheese and garlic in a bowl and gently toss. Add oregano, salt, pepper and olive oil and toss to coat. Marinate, covered, for several hours.

Variable servings

TOMATO ROSE

2 envelopes Italian salad dressing mix

6 tablespoons vegetable oil

1/4 cup rosé or sherry wine

3 tablespoons red wine vinegar

4 large tomatoes, chopped

1 (14-ounce) can artichoke hearts,
   drained, cut into halves

1 (6-ounce) can pitted black olives,
   drained

2 (4-ounce) cans button mushrooms,
   drained

Boiled fresh or canned pearl onions

Baby carrots

Whisk the dressing mix, oil, wine and vinegar in a large bowl. Add the tomatoes, artichokes, olives, mushrooms, onions and carrots and gently toss. Marinate, covered, in the refrigerator for 8 to 10 hours. You may store, covered, in the refrigerator for several days.

Serves 4 to 6

1953   *Otto Klemperer made his final appearance at the Bowl, conducting Beethoven's Ninth Symphony at the Bowl's 1,000th concert. Because he had suffered a broken hip some years before, the maestro conducted while seated in a chair.*

STUFFED TOMATOES

4 firm ripe tomatoes
Salt
1 avocado
Lemon juice
6 slices bacon, crisp-cooked, crumbled
1/4 cup minced black olives
1/4 cup fine seasoned bread crumbs
2 to 3 tablespoons minced red onion
2 to 4 tablespoons mayonnaise
Minced garlic to taste

Slice the top from each tomato. Scoop out the pulp, discarding the seeds and juice. Mince the pulp. Sprinkle the inside of each tomato shell with salt. Invert the shells on a rack to drain. Mash the avocado with the lemon juice in a bowl.

Combine the avocado, bacon, olives, bread crumbs, onion, mayonnaise, garlic and reserved pulp in a bowl and mix well. Stuff each tomato shell with some of the bacon mixture. Arrange the tomatoes in a baking pan.

Bake at 350 degrees for 20 minutes. Serve immediately or chill, covered, for 2 to 3 hours before serving. Garnish each with a sprig of fresh parsley, mint or other herbs, 1 peeled cooked shrimp, 1/2 olive or the tomato top. You may substitute 1/4 cup minced ham or 8 to 10 minced cooked shrimp for the bacon or use a combination of 2 or more.

Serves 4

1958 *In the fall, Ringling Brothers and Barnum & Bailey Circus leased the Bowl for a performance, which elicited no great objection by regular Bowl goers, who had already experienced performing animals at Western Nights, and chimps, clowns, and tumblers at Family Nights. However, the circus fared badly because of rain.*

DOLMAS

This is a very time-consuming recipe...but well worth the effort!

3 onions, chopped
1/2 cup olive oil
1 cup long grain rice
1/2 cup water
1/2 cup chopped fresh parsley
1 bunch green onions, chopped
1/4 cup pine nuts
2 tablespoons dried dillweed, or 1/2 teaspoon cinnamon
2 tablespoons lemon juice
Salt and pepper to taste
Minced garlic (optional)
1 large jar grape leaves
1 cup water
1/2 cup olive oil
2 tablespoons lemon juice

Sauté the onions in 1/2 cup olive oil in a saucepan. Stir in the rice, 1/2 cup water, parsley, green onions, pine nuts, dillweed, 2 tablespoons lemon juice, salt, pepper and garlic. Cook for 10 minutes or until the liquid is absorbed, stirring occasionally. Remove from heat. Let stand until cool.

Drain the grape leaves and gently separate. Rinse in cold water and drain. Lay flat shiny side down on a hard surface. Spread 3 of the leaves over the bottom of a 5-quart saucepan.

Spoon 1 teaspoon of the rice mixture in the center of each of the remaining grape leaves. Fold the sides of each leaf to the center and roll tightly from the stem. Arrange the rolls in compact layers in the prepared saucepan. Whisk 1 cup water, 1/2 cup olive oil and 2 tablespoons lemon juice in a bowl. Pour over the rolls. Place a plate over the rolls to prevent them from unrolling during the cooking process.

Bring to a boil; reduce the heat. Simmer for 30 minutes. Let stand until cool; do not remove the plate. Chill for 3 hours or longer before serving. You may prepare 1 day in advance and store, covered, in the refrigerator.

Makes about 3 dozen dolmades

DOC SEVERINSEN'S THIN SPAGHETTI WITH BASIL TOMATO SAUCE

1 large bunch fresh basil (preferably with smallest leaves possible)

2 cups canned Italian plum tomatoes, seeded, drained, coarsely chopped

5 large garlic cloves, finely chopped

1/3 cup (or more) olive oil

1 teaspoon salt

Freshly ground pepper (about 6 twists of the mill)

4 quarts water

Salt to taste

16 ounces spaghettini

Remove the basil leaves from the stalks, discarding the stalks. Rinse the leaves with cold water and chop. The yield should measure 1 1/2 to 2 cups. Combine the basil, tomatoes, garlic, olive oil, 1 teaspoon salt and pepper in a saucepan and mix well. Cook over medium-high heat for 15 minutes, stirring occasionally.

Bring the water and salt to taste to a boil in a large saucepan. Add the pasta: Cook until al dente; drain. Transfer the pasta to a heated bowl. Add the tomato sauce and toss to mix. Add additional olive oil if desired and mix well. Serve hot or cold.

Serves 4

1958   *Only once has a piano string broken during a performance at the Bowl. Rudolf Serkin was the victim during the first movement of Beethoven's Piano Concerto No. 5 (the "Emperor"), and the "house" piano had to be trundled out so he could finish the performance.*

PASTA WITH PESTO AND SUN-DRIED TOMATOES

16 ounces fresh or dried spiral pasta
Pesto (below)
1 (4-ounce) jar sun-dried tomatoes, drained, cut into thirds
1 (4-ounce) can sliced black olives, drained

Cook the pasta using package directions until al dente; drain. Toss the pasta with the pesto in a bowl until coated. Stir in the sun-dried tomatoes and olives. You may substitute commercially prepared pesto for the homemade pesto.

Serves 8

PESTO

2 cups fresh basil leaves
1/3 cup freshly grated Parmesan cheese or pecorino cheese
1/3 cup extra-virgin olive oil
1/4 cup pine nuts or walnuts
2 garlic cloves
1/2 teaspoon salt

Combine the basil, cheese, olive oil, pine nuts, garlic and salt in a blender or food processor container. Process until smooth.

Serves 8

PASTA REFRESHER

8 ounces rotini

1 (20-ounce) can pineapple chunks, drained

2 cups cubed melon

1 cup seedless grape halves

1 cup sliced celery

1 cup vanilla yogurt

1/4 cup mayonnaise

1/2 teaspoon ginger

Cook the pasta in boiling water in a saucepan until tender; drain. Let stand until cool. Combine the pasta, pineapple, melon, grapes and celery in a bowl and gently mix.

Mix the yogurt, mayonnaise and ginger in a bowl. Fold the yogurt mixture into the pasta mixture. Chill, covered, for 2 to 10 hours. Serve cold. You may substitute any fresh fruits for the pineapple, melon and grapes.

Serves 6 to 8

1958 *Through a fortunate coincidence, William Severns booked a young Van Cliburn to play at the Bowl prior to his winning the Tchaikovsky International Competition Award in Moscow. Severns held Cliburn to his fee of $1,250 for one performance, but then offered him a second appearance for 50 percent of the gate, for which the 21-year-old received more than $20,000!*

BASIC QUICHE

This is easiest if prepared in an 8- or 9-inch tart pan with a removable bottom, but it may be prepared in a disposable pie pan. Quiches may also be made without a crust.

Basic Crust

1/3 cup plus 3 tablespoons flour

1/8 teaspoon salt

3 tablespoons unsalted butter, chilled

1 tablespoon shortening, chilled

1 1/2 tablespoons (or more) ice water

Basic Filling

1 cup heavy cream

1 cup milk

1 1/2 cups shredded Swiss, Jarlsberg or Gruyère cheese

4 eggs, lightly beaten

For the crust, combine the flour and salt in a bowl and mix well. Cut in the butter and shortening with a pastry blender or process in a food processor until crumbly. Add the ice water and stir until an easily handled pastry forms.

Press the pastry over the bottom and up the side of a tart pan; do not roll out the dough. Bake at 425 degrees for 7 minutes or until golden brown.

For the filling, scald the heavy cream and milk in a saucepan. Let stand until cool. Whisk in the cheese and eggs. Pour the cream mixture into the pastry-lined tart pan. Bake at 375 degrees for 30 to 35 minutes or until a knife inserted in the center comes out clean.

Serves 6

BACON AND ONION QUICHE

Basic Crust (page 113)
8 ounces bacon
2 medium brown onions, chopped
Basic Filling (page 113)

Prepare and bake the Basic Crust. Fry the bacon in a skillet until crisp. Drain and crumble. Sprinkle the bacon and onions over the bottom of the baked layer. Prepare the Basic Filling. Pour into the prepared tart pan. Bake as directed on page 113.

Serves 6

WILD MUSHROOM QUICHE

3 ounces each oyster, shiitake and porcini mushrooms
3 tablespoons chopped fresh chives or scallion tops
2 tablespoons Dijon mustard
2 tablespoons red wine
2 tablespoons olive oil
1/3 cup half-and-half
2 eggs
Butter, softened
1/3 cup crumbled feta cheese, bleu cheese or goat cheese

Sauté the mushrooms, chives, Dijon mustard and wine in the olive oil in a skillet until the liquid is absorbed. Remove from heat. Whisk the half-and-half and eggs in a bowl until blended.

Coat the bottom of a disposable pie pan with butter. Sprinkle the feta cheese over the bottom. Spoon the mushroom mixture over the cheese. Pour the cream mixture over the prepared layers. Bake at 350 degrees for 25 to 30 minutes or until a knife inserted in the center comes out clean.

Serves 6

PROVENÇAL VEGETABLE QUICHE

1/2 pound eggplant, chopped

1/2 pound zucchini, chopped

1/4 pound red bell peppers, chopped

1/4 pound onions, chopped

3 tablespoons olive oil

1/4 pound tomatoes, chopped

1 large garlic clove, crushed or minced

1 tablespoon chopped fresh tarragon or basil

Salt and pepper to taste

1 cup shredded Swiss or Gruyère cheese

2/3 cup half-and-half

2 eggs

Toss the eggplant, zucchini, bell peppers, onions and olive oil in a baking dish. Bake at 375 degrees for 20 minutes, turning once. Stir in the tomatoes, garlic, tarragon, salt and pepper. Bake for 15 minutes longer, turning once.

Sprinkle the cheese over the bottom of a greased 8-inch pie plate. Spoon the vegetable mixture over the cheese. Whisk the half-and-half and eggs in a bowl until blended. Pour the egg mixture over the prepared layers. Bake at 350 degrees for 25 to 30 minutes or until a knife inserted in the center comes out clean.

Serves 6

1959 *Although jazz greats like Ella Fitzgerald, Nat King Cole, Peggy Lee, and Benny Goodman had previously appeared at the Bowl, the first Jazz Festival was a two-day postseason event featuring Count Basie, George Shearing, Sarah Vaughan, and Shorty Rogers. Later years brought the famous Newport and Playboy Jazz Festivals.*

SPINACH CHEESE PIE

1 to 2 tablespoons butter, softened

4 (10-ounce) packages frozen spinach, thawed, drained

2 bunches green onions, chopped

1 medium red bell pepper, finely chopped

$^1/_3$ cup olive oil

8 eggs

1 pound feta cheese, crumbled

$^1/_2$ cup chopped fresh parsley

1 (16-ounce) package phyllo pastry

$^1/_4$ cup ($^1/_2$ stick) butter, melted

3 tablespoons olive oil

Coat the bottom and sides of a 9x13-inch baking dish with the softened butter. Press the excess moisture from the spinach. Sauté the green onions and bell pepper in $^1/_3$ cup olive oil in a skillet for 5 minutes. Whisk the eggs in a bowl until blended. Add the spinach, green onion mixture, cheese and parsley to the eggs and mix well.

Cut 16 of the pastry sheets with scissors or a sharp knife to fit the prepared baking dish. Brush 8 sheets with a mixture of the melted butter and 3 tablespoons olive oil. Layer the sheets in the prepared baking dish. Spread the spinach mixture over the prepared layer. Top with the remaining 8 pastry sheets, brushing each with some of the butter mixture.

Brush the top layer heavily with the butter mixture and score the top 8 sheets into diamond shapes with a razor or sharp knife. Bake at 350 degrees for 45 minutes or until golden brown. Serve warm or at room temperature with Greek olives, pepperoncini, celery stalks, sliced red bell pepper and/or cherry tomatoes.

Serves 8 to 10

PERFORMING ARTS

The Theatre & Music Magazine for California and Texas

JULY 15-19   50¢

HOLLYWOOD BOWL
SUMMER FESTIVAL '86

LOS ANGELES PHILHARMONIC
André Previn, Music Director

Ernest Fleischmann, General Director
Robert Harth, Managing Director

Desserts

SOUR CREAM POUND CAKE WITH FRESH BERRIES

1 3/4 cups flour
1 cup sugar
1/2 cup (1 stick) unsalted butter,
   softened
3 eggs, lightly beaten
1 teaspoon baking soda
1 teaspoon cardamom or ginger

1/2 teaspoon cinnamon
1 cup sour cream
1 teaspoon vanilla extract
Fresh Berries à la Grand Marnier
   (below)
Sprigs of fresh mint and lemon zest

Combine the flour, sugar, unsalted butter, eggs, baking soda, cardamom and cinnamon in a food processor container. Pulse until blended, scraping the side of the container frequently; do not overblend. Add the sour cream and vanilla. Pulse to blend.

Spoon the batter into a greased and floured 5x9-inch loaf pan, striking the pan on a hard surface to remove any air bubbles. Place the pan on the center oven rack. Bake at 350 degrees for 50 to 60 minutes or until the cake springs back when lightly touched and the top is golden brown.

Run a knife around the edges of the loaf to loosen and invert onto a wire rack to cool. Slice and spoon some of the Fresh Berries à la Grand Marnier over each serving. Garnish with mint and/or lemon zest.

Serves 12

FRESH BERRIES À LA GRAND MARNIER

1 pint strawberries
1 pint blackberries

1 pint raspberries
1/2 cup Grand Marnier

Combine the strawberries, blackberries and raspberries in a bowl and gently toss. Add the Grand Marnier and stir just until coated.

Serves 12

AMERICAN FLAG STRAWBERRY SHORTCAKE

2 cups sifted flour

1/4 cup sugar

1 tablespoon baking powder

1/8 teaspoon salt

1/2 cup (1 stick) butter, cut into
   small pieces

1 egg

Milk

1 pint fresh strawberries, sliced,
   lightly sweetened

2 pints whipping cream

2 tablespoons confectioners' sugar

2 teaspoons vanilla extract

1 pint blueberries

1 pint fresh strawberries, hulled

Mix the flour, sugar, baking powder and salt in a bowl. Cut in the butter until crumbly. Whisk the egg in a 2-cup measuring cup. Add just enough milk to measure 3/4 cup and mix well.

Make a well in the center of the flour mixture. Add the egg mixture to the flour mixture and stir just until blended; the mixture should be somewhat lumpy. Or process in a food processor just until blended. Pat the dough over the bottom of a greased 10x15-inch baking sheet with sides. Bake at 400 degrees for 15 to 20 minutes or until a wooden pick inserted in the dough comes out clean. Cool in pan on a wire rack.

Spread the sliced strawberries evenly over the baked layer. Beat 1 pint of the whipping cream in a mixing bowl until soft peaks form. Add 1 tablespoon of the confectioners' sugar and 1 teaspoon of the vanilla and mix well. Spread the whipped cream over the strawberries.

Arrange the blueberries densely in the upper left quadrant of the cake to form a field of blue. Place the hulled strawberries pointed ends up in rows to form the stripes; make the rows fairly close.

Beat the remaining 1 pint of whipping cream in a mixing bowl until soft peaks form. Add the remaining 1 tablespoon confectioners' sugar and remaining 1 teaspoon vanilla and mix well. Spoon the whipped cream into a pastry bag fitted with a rosette tip. Pipe stars onto the field of blueberries. Change the rosette tip to a pastry tip. Make generous white stripes between the rows of strawberries. Extra whipped cream may be used to pipe around the edges of the cake. Chill, covered, until serving time.

Serves 36

NUTMEG CAKE FROM SYRIA

2 cups packed light or dark
  brown sugar
2 cups sifted flour
1/2 cup (1 stick) butter or margarine
1 cup sour cream

1 egg
1 teaspoon nutmeg
1 teaspoon baking soda
1/2 cup chopped walnuts
Middle East Oranges (below)

Combine the brown sugar and flour in a bowl and mix well. Cut in the butter until crumbly. Pat half the crumb mixture over the bottom of a 9x9-inch cake pan. Stir the sour cream, egg, nutmeg and baking soda into the remaining crumb mixture. Spoon the sour cream mixture over the prepared layer. Sprinkle with the walnuts.

    Bake at 350 degrees for 35 to 40 minutes or until the edges pull from the sides of the pan. Cool in pan on a wire rack. Cut into squares. Serve with Middle East Oranges.

Serves 9

MIDDLE EAST ORANGES

6 large navel oranges
1 tablespoon orange flower water
1 tablespoon confectioners' sugar

3/4 teaspoon cinnamon
Sliced almonds, toasted
Fresh mint leaves

Peel the oranges and remove the white pith. Cut the oranges into thin slices. Arrange the slices in a serving dish. Sprinkle with the orange flower water. You may prepare up to this point 1 hour in advance and chill, covered, in the refrigerator.

    Sprinkle a mixture of the confectioners' sugar and cinnamon over the orange slices just before serving. Top with almonds and garnish with mint leaves. Orange flower water is a flavoring extract that is available at liquor stores and in the specialty food section of many supermarkets.

Serves 9

ANISE BISCOTTI

2 cups sugar

1 cup (2 sticks) butter or margarine, melted

$1/4$ cup anise seeds

$1/4$ cup anise extract

2 cups coarsely chopped almonds

6 eggs, lightly beaten

$5^1/2$ cups flour

1 tablespoon baking powder

Combine the sugar, butter, anise seeds and flavoring in a bowl and mix well. Stir in the almonds. Add the eggs and beat until mixed. Stir in a mixture of the flour and baking powder. Chill, covered, for 2 to 3 hours.

   Grease several baking sheets. Shape the dough on the prepared baking sheets into flat loaves about $1/2$ inch thick, 2 inches wide and as long as the baking sheet. Arrange no more than 2 loaves parallel and well apart on each baking sheet. Bake at 375 degrees for 20 minutes.

   Cool the loaves on the baking sheets until they can be comfortably touched. Cut each loaf diagonally into $1/2$- to $3/4$-inch-thick slices. Arrange the slices cut side up on the baking sheets. Bake at 375 degrees for 15 minutes or until light brown. Remove to a wire rack to cool. Store in an airtight container.

Makes 9 dozen

PEANUT BUTTER BARS

1 1/4 cups sugar

1/3 cup butter, softened

1 cup peanut butter

3 eggs

1 teaspoon vanilla extract

1 cup flour

1/4 teaspoon salt

1 1/4 cups chocolate chips

Beat the sugar and butter in a mixing bowl until creamy, scraping the bowl occasionally. Add the peanut butter. Beat until blended. Add the eggs 1 at a time, beating well after each addition. Stir in the vanilla. Add a mixture of the flour and salt and mix well. Stir in 1/2 cup of the chocolate chips.

Spread the batter on a nonstick baking sheet with sides or in a 9×13-inch baking pan. Bake at 350 degrees for 25 to 30 minutes or until golden brown and firm to the touch. Sprinkle the remaining chocolate chips over the baked layer. Let stand until the chocolate chips melt and then spread evenly over the top. Let stand until set. Cut into bars.

Makes 3 dozen bars

1961   *Judy Garland was not deterred by wet weather. Nor was her audience! In a pouring rain, she sang a full concert standing on a ramp extended out over the reflecting pool. Due to Southern California's obliging weather, only six concerts in 80 years have had to be canceled because of rain.*

NANCY SILVERTON AND MARK PEEL'S CHEWY CHOCOLATE CHIP COOKIES

Campanile Restaurant is famous for these cookies!

8 ounces chocolate, coarsely chopped (Valrhona is the best)

2 1/2 cups flour

1/2 teaspoon baking soda

1/4 teaspoon baking powder

1 cup (2 sticks) plus 2 tablespoons unsalted butter, softened

1 cup sugar

3/4 cup packed brown sugar

1 egg

1 teaspoon vanilla extract

1 cup chopped walnuts

Chill the chocolate in the refrigerator for 2 to 3 hours. Sift the flour, baking soda and baking powder into a bowl and mix well. Using the paddle attachment of an electric mixer, beat the unsalted butter in a mixing bowl at medium speed for 3 to 5 minutes or until light and fluffy. Add the sugar and brown sugar. Beat until blended.

Whisk the egg and vanilla in a bowl until blended. Add the egg mixture to the creamed mixture and beat until blended, scraping the side of the bowl occasionally. Add half the flour mixture and beat until blended. Add the remaining flour mixture and beat just until combined. Beat in the walnuts and chocolate. Chill the dough, wrapped in plastic wrap, for 2 hours or until firm.

Line a cookie sheet with cooking parchment. Shape the dough into 1 1/2-inch balls and arrange the balls 2 inches apart on the prepared cookie sheet. Press each ball lightly with the palm of your hand. Bake at 325 degrees for 8 to 10 minutes or until the cookies have risen and cracked; do not overbake. Cool on cookie sheet for 2 minutes. Remove to a wire rack to cool completely. Store in an airtight container.

Makes 2 to 3 dozen cookies

BOB HOPE'S FAVORITE LEMON PIE

1 cup sugar

3 tablespoons cornstarch

1 cup boiling water

4 egg yolks, lightly beaten

1/4 cup lemon juice

2 tablespoons butter

Grated zest of 1 lemon

1/8 teaspoon salt

1 baked (9-inch) pie shell

3 egg whites

2 tablespoons sugar

Combine 1 cup sugar and cornstarch in a saucepan and mix well. Add the boiling water gradually, stirring constantly. Cook until thickened and smooth, stirring constantly.

Stir a small amount of the hot mixture into the egg yolks; stir the egg yolks into the hot mixture. Add the lemon juice, butter, lemon zest and salt and mix well. Cook for 2 to 3 minutes, stirring constantly. Spoon the lemon filling into the pie shell.

Beat the egg whites in a mixing bowl until soft peaks form. Add 2 tablespoons sugar gradually, beating constantly until stiff peaks form. Spread the meringue over the lemon filling, sealing to the edge. Bake at 350 degrees for 15 minutes or until light brown.

Serves 6 to 8

1961 *Zubin Mehta made his Bowl debut at the age of 25. "I don't think there has been an important artist in the twentieth century, classical or popular, who has not enthralled thousands at the Hollywood Bowl," Mehta said. "It is as American as apple pie." On trips to Europe, he and Philharmonic Board member William Connell negotiated the purchase of rare instruments for the orchestra, including several Stradivari and Guarneri, which are used by several of the orchestra's first chair players.*

COOL PECAN MOCHA PIE

6 ounces semisweet chocolate

1/2 teaspoon instant coffee granules

2 eggs, beaten

1/4 cup sifted confectioners' sugar

3 tablespoons Kahlúa

3/4 cup whipping cream, whipped

1 teaspoon vanilla extract

Pecan Crust (below)

3/4 cup whipping cream

1 tablespoon Kahlúa

Grated semisweet chocolate

Combine 6 ounces chocolate and coffee granules in a double boiler over simmering water. Cook until the chocolate melts, stirring frequently. Add about 1/4 of the hot chocolate mixture to the eggs; stir the eggs into the hot mixture. Stir in the confectioners' sugar and 3 tablespoons Kahlúa.

Cook until a candy thermometer registers 165 degrees, stirring constantly. Cool to room temperature. Fold 3/4 cup whipped whipping cream into the chocolate mixture. Stir in the vanilla. Spoon the chocolate filling into the Pecan Crust.

Freeze, covered, for 8 hours. To serve, thaw the pie in the refrigerator for 1 hour. Beat 3/4 cup whipping cream in a mixing bowl until soft peaks form. Add 1 tablespoon Kahlúa gradually and mix well. Spread the whipped cream over the chocolate filling, sealing to the edge. Sprinkle with grated chocolate.

Serves 6 to 8

PECAN CRUST

1 3/4 cups finely chopped pecans

1/3 cup packed brown sugar

3 tablespoons butter, melted

2 teaspoons Kahlúa

Combine the pecans, brown sugar, butter and Kahlúa in a bowl and mix well. Press the crumb mixture over the bottom and side of a 9-inch pie plate with the back of a spoon. Bake at 350 degrees for 10 to 12 minutes or until light brown.

Makes 1 pie crust

POACHED PEAR TART

This beautiful to look at and beautiful to eat tart is a fitting finale to your picnic. From renowned restaurateur Piero Selvaggio of Valentino.

Amaretti Crust

3/4 cup flour

1/4 cup fine amaretti cookie crumbs

1 tablespoon sugar

7 tablespoons butter, chilled, cut into
   tablespoons

1/4 cup ice water

Pear Fillling

4 large firm pears, peeled,
   cut into halves

1 fifth cabernet sauvignon

1 1/2 cups (3 sticks) unsalted butter

6 eggs

2 cups sugar

1/2 cup plus 2 tablespoons flour

4 teaspoons vanilla extract

For the crust, combine the flour, cookie crumbs and sugar in a food processor fitted with a metal blade. Process until mixed. Add the butter 1 tablespoon at a time, processing constantly until of the consistency of oats. Add the ice water gradually, processing constantly until the mixture forms a ball.

Roll the dough on a lightly floured surface to fit a 10-inch tart pan with removable bottom. Fit the dough into the tart pan and trim the edge. Freeze, covered with foil or plastic wrap, until needed or for up to 1 week.

Line the bottom of the prepared tart pan with foil. Weight the foil with dried beans. Bake at 375 degrees for 12 minutes. Discard the beans and foil. Let stand until cool.

For the filling, combine the pears and wine in a saucepan. Bring to a boil; reduce the heat. Simmer for 20 to 30 minutes or just until the pears are tender. Cool in wine; drain. To enhance the wine flavor, store the pears in the wine in the refrigerator for up to 4 days before using.

Heat the butter in a heavy skillet over medium heat for 1 to 2 minutes or until the butter comes to a boil, brown flecks form and the foam is light golden, stirring constantly. Remove from heat.

Whisk the eggs in a bowl until blended. Stir in the sugar and flour. Add the butter to the egg mixture, whisking constantly. Hot butter will bubble at first. Keep mixing! The mixture will be mustard/tan in color with flecks and very viscous, but pourable. Add the vanilla and beat until smooth.

Spoon the filling over the baked crust. Arrange the pear halves in a circle in alternating directions. Bake at 400 degrees for 30 minutes or until set.

Serves 8 to 10

WALNUT TORTE

For those whose weakness is anything chocolaty, nutty, and chewy, this is the apple the Serpent holds out. Disguised as a torte, it's really a two-pound inch-thick chocolate-coated candy bar from Chef Ken Frank, chef/owner of La Toque Restaurant in Napa Valley.

$2^1/4$ cups sugar

$2/3$ cup water

$2/3$ cup heavy cream

14 tablespoons ($1^3/4$ sticks) unsalted
  butter

$2^3/4$ cups coarsely chopped walnuts

Pâte Sucrée (page 129)

1 egg, beaten

6 ounces bittersweet chocolate

6 tablespoons heavy cream

Mix the sugar and water in a saucepan. Brush down the side of the saucepan with a wet pastry brush to force down any sugar crystals. Cook over medium heat until the sugar is caramelized and a deep golden brown in color, occasionally brushing the side of the saucepan with a clean wet pastry brush to prevent crystallization; do not stir or shake the saucepan during the cooking process. Remove from heat. Stir in $2/3$ cup heavy cream and unsalted butter with a wooden spoon. Do at arm's length, for the sugar may pop. Add the walnuts, stirring until coated. Let stand until cool.

Remove the Pâte Sucrée from the refrigerator. Knead until soft, but do not overwork. Dust the work surface lightly with flour. Roll $2/3$ of the dough into an 11-inch circle approximately $1/8$ inch thick, reserving the excess dough. Roll the circle loosely on the rolling pin and unroll over a 9-inch tart pan. Press the dough carefully over the bottom and up the side of the pan. Trim the top, leaving a $1/2$-inch overhang. Roll the remaining dough and reserved scraps into a 9-inch circle, $1/8$ inch thick.

Pour the warm caramelized filling into the prepared tart pan. Brush the overhang with the egg. Arrange the 9-inch dough circle over the top of the filling. Crimp the edge tightly, pinching off any large overlapping pieces. Make 4 to 5 vents in the top with a sharp knife. Bake on a baking sheet at 350 degrees for 25 to 30 minutes or until golden brown. Let stand until room temperature. Chill in the refrigerator.

Heat the chocolate and 6 tablespoons heavy cream in a double boiler until warm but not hot. Stir until smooth and shiny. Cut a 9-inch circle of corrugated cardboard. Invert the chilled tart onto the cardboard, remove the pan and place the tart on a wire rack. Pour the chocolate mixture over the tart and spread over the top and side. Chill until 30 minutes before serving.

Serves 8 to 12

PATE SUCREE

1³/4 cups plus 2 tablespoons flour

10 tablespoons plus 1 teaspoon unsalted butter

3¹/2 tablespoons sugar

¹/8 teaspoon salt

2 egg yolks

1 tablespoon water

4 drops of vanilla extract

Combine the flour, unsalted butter, sugar and salt in a food processor bowl. Process for 45 seconds. Add the egg yolks, water and vanilla. Process for 30 seconds longer or until the mixture forms a ball. Add additional water if needed. The dough should be smooth but not sticky.

Wrap the dough in plastic wrap. Chill for 4 to 5 hours or preferably overnight.

Makes 1 crust

1962 *Two moving sidewalks were constructed to serve 75 percent of the audience area. Capacity was estimated at 8,000 people per hour. Two more were added later, and in 1998, escalators replaced the three upper moving sidewalks.*

CHOCOLATE MOUSSE

1 1/2 cups semisweet chocolate chips
1/4 cup strong coffee
7 egg yolks
1/4 cup sugar

1 teaspoon vanilla extract
7 egg whites
1/8 teaspoon salt
Vanilla Custard Sauce (below)

Heat the chocolate chips in a double boiler over hot water until melted, stirring frequently. Stir in the coffee. Let stand until cool.

Beat the egg yolks in a mixing bowl until thick and pale yellow. Add the sugar and vanilla. Beat until blended. Add the chocolate mixture to the egg yolk mixture and beat until smooth.

Combine the egg whites and salt in a mixing bowl. Beat until soft peaks begin to form; do not overbeat. Fold the chocolate mixture into the egg whites. Spoon into a lightly greased 1 1/2-quart mold. Chill until firm.

Invert the mold onto a dessert plate with sides or into a shallow bowl. Pour the Vanilla Custard Sauce around the mousse. You may serve in individual custard or soufflé cups or in Champagne or wine glasses. The Vanilla Custard Sauce may be passed separately. To avoid raw eggs that may carry salmonella, we suggest using an equivalent amount of pasteurized egg substitute.

Serves 8 to 10

VANILLA CUSTARD SAUCE

2 cups milk
3 eggs
6 tablespoons sugar

1/4 teaspoon salt
1 teaspoon vanilla extract

Scald the milk in a double boiler over hot water. Remove from heat. Whisk the eggs, sugar and salt until blended. Add the scalded milk gradually, whisking constantly. Return the milk mixture to the double boiler.

Cook over simmering water until the mixture coats a metal spoon, stirring constantly. Remove from heat. Set over a pan of ice water until cooled. Stir in the vanilla. Chill, covered, until serving time.

Serves 8 to 10

LEMON MOUSSE WITH KIWIFRUIT

1 tablespoon unflavored gelatin

1/4 cup cold water

3/4 cup superfine sugar

4 egg yolks

4 egg whites

1 cup whipping cream

Grated zest and juice of 1 lemon

1/2 cup apricot preserves

2 tablespoons water

2 kiwifruit, sliced

Sprinkle the gelatin over the cold water in a heatproof measuring cup. Let stand for 5 minutes to soften. Place the cup in a small saucepan. Add enough boiling water to the saucepan to measure 1 inch. Cook over low heat until the gelatin dissolves, stirring constantly.

Beat the sugar and egg yolks in a mixing bowl until thick and pale yellow. Beat the egg whites in a mixing bowl until stiff peaks form. Beat the whipping cream in a mixing bowl until stiff peaks form.

Add the gelatin mixture to the egg yolk mixture and mix well. Stir in the lemon zest and lemon juice. Fold in the egg whites and then fold in the whipped cream. Spoon the mousse into a porcelain soufflé dish. Chill, covered, for 8 to 10 hours.

Combine the preserves and water in a saucepan. Cook over medium heat until heated through and of a glaze consistency, stirring frequently. Force the glaze through a fine sieve into a bowl. Dip the sliced kiwifruit in the glaze. Arrange the slices in a decorative pattern over the mousse. To avoid eggs that may carry salmonella, we suggest using an equivalent amount of pasteurized egg substitute.

Serves 8

1964   *Has there ever been a more prominent date in pop culture than August 23, 1964? On that date, the Beatles appeared at the Bowl. With a single ad and one blurb on a teenager TV station, 18,000 tickets were sold in April. Throughout their concert, noise from screaming fans overpowered any sound coming from the stage.*

TIRAMISU

1 1/2 cups whipping cream

1 cup espresso or strong coffee

3 tablespoons Cognac or rum

1 teaspoon vanilla extract

1 cup sifted confectioners' sugar

8 ounces mascarpone cheese

1 (8-ounce) package ladyfingers

2 tablespoons baking cocoa

Combine the whipping cream, 1 tablespoon of the espresso, Cognac and vanilla in a chilled mixing bowl. Beat at high speed until thick but not stiff. Beat the confectioners' sugar and cheese in a mixing bowl just until smooth. Add a heaping spoonful of the whipped cream mixture and mix well. Add the remaining whipped cream mixture 1/2 at a time, stirring gently but thoroughly after each addition to remove lumps. Do not overbeat or the cheese may separate.

Dip the ladyfingers in the remaining espresso and cut if needed to fit the serving dish. Arrange the ladyfingers, whipped cream mixture and baking cocoa 1/3 at a time in an 8×8-inch dish. Chill, covered, until serving time.

Serves 6 to 8

1966 *The 21-year-old Itzhak Perlman, not yet a superstar, made his Bowl debut; he has returned to appreciative audiences many times since. Perlman's rapport with the Bowl's huge audiences is felt across the footlights, making him one of the Bowl's favorite artists.*

SUMMER FIGS WITH LEMON AND PEPPERMINT COULIS

One of summer's most luscious fruits is given an extra tang in this recipe from Pinot Bistro, created by Octavio Becerra.

1 tablespoon sugar
1 teaspoon fresh lemon juice
1 teaspoon water
6 tops fresh peppermint (young tender leaves only)
12 fresh ripe summer figs, cut into quarters

Heat the sugar in a small saucepan over high heat until caramelized. Stir in the lemon juice and water. Simmer for about 5 minutes, stirring occasionally. Chop 2 of the peppermint tops and infuse with the caramelized sugar. Let stand until cool. Drizzle the sauce over the figs on a serving platter. Garnish with the remaining peppermint tops. Serve at room temperature.

Serves 4 to 6

PINEAPPLE RICE DESSERT

1 (8-ounce) can pineapple tidbits
1/4 cup each packed brown sugar and raisins
1 teaspoon butter
3/4 teaspoon vanilla extract
1/2 teaspoon salt
1/4 teaspoon cinnamon
1 1/3 cups instant rice

Drain the pineapple, reserving the juice. Add enough water to the reserved juice to measure 1 1/3 cups. Pour the pineapple juice mixture into a saucepan. Stir in the pineapple, brown sugar, raisins, butter, vanilla, salt and cinnamon. Bring the pineapple mixture to a boil. Stir in the rice. Simmer, covered, for 10 minutes. Spoon into dessert goblets. Serve warm or cold.

Serves 4 to 6

JOACHIM SPLICHAL'S CLAFOUTIS OF SUMMER PEACHES "PERE ANDRE"

Pastry

1 7/8 cups flour

2 tablespoons vanilla sugar or
    granulated sugar

1/2 teaspoon salt

2/3 cup plus 1 tablespoon butter,
    chilled, cut into 1/2-inch pieces

1 egg, lightly beaten

1 to 3 tablespoons ice water

Peach Filling

1/2 cup plus 1 tablespoon sugar

1/2 cup each heavy cream and milk

4 eggs

3 tablespoons flour

1/4 cup (1/2 stick) unsalted butter

5 large or 7 medium peaches,
    peeled, cut into quarters

1/4 cup sugar

For the pastry, combine the flour, sugar and salt in a food processor bowl. Process until mixed. Add the butter. Pulse 3 or 4 times or until the butter is the size of large bread crumbs. Do not overprocess.

Drizzle half the egg and 1 tablespoon of the ice water over the flour mixture. Pulse for a few seconds. Add the remaining egg and 1 more tablespoon of the ice water. Process for 5 to 10 seconds or until the mixture comes together in a ball on the central column. If this does not happen, add the remaining 1 tablespoon ice water and process. Shape the pastry into a ball on a sheet of plastic wrap. Chill, covered with plastic wrap, for 1 to 2 hours.

Butter and line a nonstick 9x9-inch baking pan or a springform pan with baking parchment. Roll the pastry 1/8 inch thick on a lightly floured hard surface. Pat the pastry over the bottom and partially up the sides of the prepared pan to prevent the pastry from sagging down into the pan. Chill for 45 minutes. Pierce the bottom of the pie pastry with a fork and line the bottom with baking parchment. Weight the baking parchment with dried beans. Bake at 350 degrees for 15 minutes. Discard the beans and baking parchment.

For the filling, combine the sugar, heavy cream, milk, eggs and flour in a blender container. Process until smooth. Heat the unsalted butter in a small sauté pan over medium heat. Stir in the peaches and sugar. Cook for 4 to 5 minutes or until the peaches are tender and slightly caramelized. Pour a small amount of the batter into the pastry-lined baking pan. Arrange the peaches over the batter. Top with the remaining batter. Bake at 350 degrees for 1 hour or just until firm. Cool slightly on a wire rack. Serve warm or at room temperature.

Serves 9

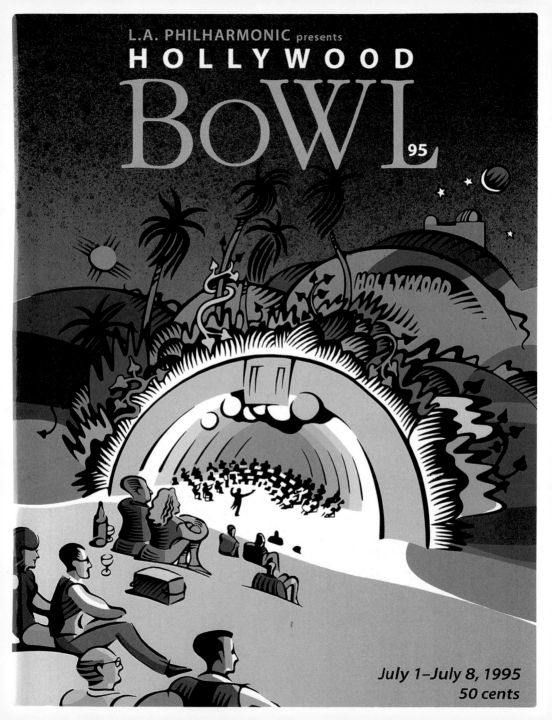

...and More

ESA-PEKKA SALONEN'S GRAVLAX WITH MUSTARD SAUCE

Salmon

1 (1 1/2- to 2-pound) salmon fillet
   with skin

3 tablespoons sea salt

1 tablespoon salt

1 tablespoon sugar

10 white peppercorns,
   coarsely ground

1/2 cup dried fennel

1/2 cup dried dillweed

Mustard Sauce

2 tablespoons Dijon mustard

2 tablespoons prepared mustard

2 tablespoons sugar

3 tablespoons white wine vinegar

1 cup vegetable oil

Salt and white pepper to taste

For the salmon, remove all the bones from the fillet. Arrange the fillet skin side down in a shallow dish. Combine the sea salt, salt and sugar in a bowl and mix well. Rub the fillet on both sides with the salt mixture. Sprinkle with the peppercorns and a mixture of the fennel and dillweed. Marinate, covered, in the refrigerator for 24 hours.

Remove the fillet from the refrigerator just before serving; do not remove the herbs. Cut the fillet diagonally into narrow strips.

For the sauce, combine the Dijon mustard, prepared mustard and sugar in a bowl and mix well. Stir in the vinegar. Add the oil gradually, whisking constantly until blended. Serve the salmon with the sauce, dark bread, beer and cold schnapps.

Wine Selection: Kendall-Jackson Grand Reserve Sauvignon Blanc

Serves 6 to 8

1969 *Ernest Fleischmann was hired as general director of the Hollywood Bowl and executive director of the Los Angeles Philharmonic, and he immediately established a now-hallowed tradition: the Tchaikovsky Spectacular with real fireworks.*

A Summer Supper from Betty and John Mauceri

John Mauceri is the principal conductor of the Hollywood Bowl Orchestra.

Gazpacho
Curried Rice Salad (page 139)
Stuffed Chicken Breasts (below)
Cold asparagus with Parmesan cheese
Baby spinach salad with mango, papaya and avocado
Fruit torte

★ ★ ★ ★ ★ ★ ★ ★ ★ ★ ★ ★ ★ ★ ★ ★ ★ ★ ★ ★

Stuffed Chicken Breasts

3 whole chicken breasts, boned
Salt and pepper to taste
1 1/2 cups chilled prepared stuffing
Paprika to taste
1 large onion, coarsely chopped

Pound the chicken flat with a mallet. Remove and discard the skin. Season the inside of the chicken with salt and pepper. Place 1/2 cup stuffing on each piece of chicken. Fold the chicken around the stuffing, enclosing the stuffing. Shape into ovals. Place seam side down in a baking pan. Sprinkle with paprika. Scatter the onion around the pan. Pour in just enough water to cover the bottom of the pan.

Bake, covered with foil, at 350 degrees for 20 minutes. Bake, uncovered, for 20 to 30 minutes or until the chicken is cooked through. Do not add more water to the pan. Remove the chicken to a plate. Chill, covered, overnight. Slice at home or at the picnic. Serve with cranberry relish.

Serves 6 (or 4 with leftovers)

CURRIED RICE SALAD

Best if prepared one day in advance.

1 onion, coarsely chopped
Olive oil
1 garlic clove, minced
1 apple, peeled, cored, coarsely chopped
1 to 2 tablespoons curry powder, or to taste
2 cups cooked rice
Salt and pepper to taste
1/2 cup raisins, or to taste
1/4 cup slivered almonds, or to taste
Chopped scallions

Sauté the onion in olive oil in a skillet until translucent. Add the garlic, apple and curry powder. Cook until tender, adding additional olive oil if needed. This is the dressing for the rice, so enough oil is needed to distribute through the rice.

Place the rice in a large bowl. Add the apple mixture and toss well. The rice will turn yellow. Add a small amount of olive oil at a time if needed. Season with salt and pepper. Add the raisins and almonds and toss well. Chill, covered, overnight. Garnish with scallions.

Serves 6

1970 *The 50th Easter Sunrise Service bloomed at the Bowl on March 29, with a double quartet of trumpeters, a 150-voice Youth Chorus in the traditional Living Cross, celebrity soloists and readers, a 180-voice Chorale, and three religious leaders officiating—a dramatic change from the lone trumpeter, Community Sing, and single pastor of the first Easter Sunrise Service on Olive Hill in 1920.*

A Spanish Tapas Picnic

Created and developed by Lois Petrovich, Cookbook Chair 1991-1999.

The robust Mediterranean flavors of this Spanish Tapas menu will satisfy a large crowd, and all the dishes can be prepared ahead. In fact, the appetizers are a picnic in themselves. To transport and serve, place all the items except the omelet and truffles in sealable plastic bags.

Appetizers

Spicy marinated shrimp	*Salami*
Sautéed roasted red peppers	*Pepperoncini*
Marinated olives	*Ripe olives*
Armenian string cheese	*Radishes*
Kasseri cheese	*Celery*
Montrachet cheese	*Sheepherder's bread*

Main Course

Orange Roasted Chicken Breasts (page 141)
Potato Omelet (page 142)
Green Bean and Hearts of Palm Salads with Classic Vinaigrette (page 143)
Sliced garden tomatoes

Dessert

Chocolate Truffles with Candied Orange Peel (page 144)

★ ★ ★ ★ ★ ★ ★ ★ ★ ★ ★ ★ ★ ★ ★ ★ ★ ★ ★

ORANGE ROASTED CHICKEN BREASTS

3 large whole chicken breasts, quartered, bone in

2 garlic cloves, pressed

2 large oranges

1 tablespoon chopped fresh thyme, or $^1/2$ tablespoon dried thyme

2 tablespoons olive oil

1$^1/2$ tablespoons honey

Salt and freshly ground pepper to taste

Place the chicken in a 9x13-inch glass baking dish. Sprinkle with garlic. Squeeze the juice of 1 orange over the chicken. Slice the oranges; cut the slices into halves. Sprinkle the chicken with thyme. Place half the orange slices under and over the chicken; reserve the remaining slices for a garnish. Drizzle with olive oil.

Bake at 375 degrees for 30 minutes, basting once. Spoon the honey over the chicken. Bake for 30 minutes longer, basting 2 to 3 times. Season with salt and pepper. Remove from the oven. Let stand until cool.

Gently pull the chicken from the bones. Place in sealable plastic bags. Add the pan drippings to the plastic bag. At the picnic site, garnish with the reserved orange slices and sprigs of fresh thyme. Serve at room temperature.

Serves 6

1971 *In a switch from the previous year's mixed musical offerings on a single night, which elicited many complaints, Tuesday and Thursday nights were designated for classical music, Saturday nights for tried-and-true favorites, Friday nights for rock and folk concerts, and Wednesday nights for Mini-Marathons. The Mini-Marathons (music played continuously for five hours, 6:00-11:00 p.m., and "admission $1.00 for whenever you come and as long as you care to stay") were introduced by general director Ernest Fleischmann in 1970. There was a Bach Marathon, a Mozart Marathon, a Stravinsky Marathon, and so on.*

POTATO OMELET

3 large baking potatoes, peeled
1 medium onion
1/2 cup extra-virgin olive oil
3 eggs, beaten
Salt and freshly ground pepper to taste

Cut the potatoes and onion into 1/8-inch slices. Toss the potatoes and onion with the olive oil in a 9-inch round microwave-safe dish. Microwave on High for 20 minutes or just until the vegetables are tender, stirring occasionally. Drain, reserving the oil. Cool for 15 minutes. Add the eggs, salt and pepper to the potato mixture and gently toss to distribute the eggs evenly.

Heat 2 tablespoons of the reserved oil in a 9- or 10-inch heavy skillet until smoking. Pour the egg mixture into the hot skillet, tilting the skillet to ensure even coverage. Cook over medium heat until the bottom begins to brown, shaking the skillet occasionally.

Invert the omelet onto a plate. Add 1 tablespoon of the reserved oil to the skillet. Slide the omelet into the skillet on the opposite side and shake the skillet. Cook until the omelet begins to brown. Invert back and forth a few more times or until the omelet holds it shape and is light brown. Cut into wedges and serve.

Serves 6

1973   *A young Luciano Pavarotti stole the show in his first local appearance singing Rodolfo in a semistaged production of* La Boheme. *He returned in 1982, a full-fledged superstar.*

GREEN BEAN AND HEARTS OF PALM SALADS

1 1/4 pounds young green beans, trimmed
1 small red onion, sliced, separated into rings
Classic Vinaigrette (below)
2 (15-ounce) cans hearts of palm, drained, cut into 1/2-inch pieces

Plunge the beans into a generous amount of boiling water in a saucepan. Return to a boil. Boil for 4 minutes or until al dente; drain. Plunge the beans into a bowl of ice water to stop the cooking process; drain. Let stand until cool.

Toss the beans and onion rings with half the vinaigrette in a bowl. Toss the hearts of palm with the remaining vinaigrette in a bowl. Place each salad in a sealable plastic bag and seal tightly. Serve at room temperature.

Serves 6 to 8

CLASSIC VINAIGRETTE

1/4 cup red wine vinegar
2 tablespoons lemon juice
1/4 teaspoon salt
1/4 teaspoon sugar
1/8 teaspoon dry mustard
1/8 teaspoon cayenne pepper
1/8 teaspoon freshly ground black pepper
1/2 cup extra-virgin olive oil

Combine the vinegar, lemon juice, salt, sugar, dry mustard, cayenne pepper and black pepper in a bowl and mix well. Add the olive oil gradually, whisking constantly until blended.

Makes 3/4 cup

CHOCOLATE TRUFFLES WITH CANDIED ORANGE PEEL

Truffles

12 ounces Belgian or other European
    semisweet chocolate

1/4 cup water

3/4 cup (11/2 sticks) butter, cut into
    pieces

2 egg yolks, lightly beaten

1/4 cup confectioners' sugar

Orange Peel

1 orange

1/2 cup sugar

1/3 cup water

For the truffles, finely grate 4 ounces of the chocolate and set aside. Heat the remaining chocolate and water in a double boiler over hot water until the chocolate melts; do not stir. Remove from heat. Add the butter gradually, mixing until smooth and shiny after each addition. Stir in the egg yolks and confectioners' sugar. Chill, covered, for 3 hours.

Roll the chocolate mixture into 11/2-inch balls with cold hands. Roll the balls twice in the reserved grated chocolate. They will become rounder each time. Remove to a tray lined with waxed paper. Chill until firm.

For the orange peel, using a zester cut 12 thin strips of the orange peel. Combine the peel, sugar and water in a saucepan. Bring to a boil. Boil for 20 minutes, stirring occasionally and adding additional water if needed. Remove the peel to a sheet of waxed paper using a slotted spoon. Let stand until cool. Serve with the truffles.

Serves 12

1979 *The first Playboy Jazz Festival was presented at the Bowl. The following year, the Bowl launched its own Jazz at the Bowl, which showcased such artists as Chick Corea, Ray Brown, Mel Tormé, Carmen McRae, and Joe Williams.*

DEBORAH BORDA'S CHERRYWOOD-SMOKED ATLANTIC SALMON

3 pounds Atlantic salmon

1 pound Eastern mussels

1 tablespoon extra-virgin olive oil

Salt and white pepper to taste

2 tablespoons cherrywood or
    other hardwood flakes (alder,
    maple or oak)

Cucumber slices

Lemon slices

Sprigs of dillweed

Wasabi Mayonnaise (below)

Rinse the salmon and mussels with cold water and pat dry with paper towels. Rub the salmon with the olive oil. Sprinkle with salt and white pepper.

Place the cherrywood flakes in the bottom of a stove-top smoker. Arrange the salmon on the rack and surround with the mussels. Smoke, covered, over low to medium heat for 25 to 30 minutes. Remove the smoker from the heat and slide the lid open. Let stand until cool.

Discard 1/2 of each mussel shell, reserving the half with the mussel. Arrange the salmon on a platter. Garnish with cucumber slices, lemon slices and sprigs of fresh dillweed. Surround the salmon with the mussels. Serve with the Wasabi Mayonnaise.

Wine Selection: Kendall-Jackson Grand Reserve Pinot Noir

Serves 12 to 15

WASABI MAYONNAISE

1 cup homemade or commercially
    prepared mayonnaise

1 to 2 tablespoons wasabi

1 tablespoon fresh lemon juice

1 tablespoon Dijon mustard

Mix the mayonnaise, wasabi, lemon juice and Dijon mustard in a bowl. Chill, covered, until serving time. You may prepare 1 to 2 days in advance and store, covered, in the refrigerator.

Makes 1 1/4 cups

LYNN HARRELL'S MAGICAL PICNIC

"The first sunny weekend in London, I rushed into Regent's Park behind the Royal Academy of Music—my picnic? Some squashed sandwiches, soggy hard-cooked eggs, and melted Twix bars. Since then, I have discovered the wonderful Villandry who produce magical picnics so that now we dine with delicious pleasure under the summer's chestnut trees and wild honeysuckle."

Lynn Harrell, Cellist

Charcuterie
   Rolled ham and salami
   Broiled or grilled sausage, sliced
   Cornichons
   Crudités
Mixed bread rolls
Venetian Sole (page 147)
Mixed leaf salad
Pansanella Salad (page 148)
Selection of cheeses
Mixed berry fruit tartlets

★ ★ ★ ★ ★ ★ ★ ★ ★ ★ ★ ★ ★ ★ ★ ★ ★ ★ ★ ★

VENETIAN SOLE

Cod or Dover sole may also be used as an alternative to lemon sole.

2 pounds lemon sole fillets, 1/2 to
   3/4 inch thick, skinned
Seasoned flour
3 beaten eggs
Fine bread crumbs
1/4 cup raisins
1 onion, thinly sliced
1/4 cup olive oil
5 bay leaves

1/2 cup white Champagne vinegar
2 tablespoons sugar
2 crushed garlic cloves
Salt and freshly ground pepper
1 cup water
Canola oil
3 tablespoons pine nuts
Chopped flat-leaf parsley

Place sole in seasoned flour, then eggs and finally bread crumbs. Lay on a tray with greaseproof paper to prevent pieces sticking together.

Cook raisins in a little water in a saucepan until they are puffy and juicy, about 15 minutes. Drain and set aside.

Soften the onion in the olive oil in a saucepan until translucent. Add bay leaves, vinegar, sugar, garlic, salt and pepper. Add the water and simmer for 30 minutes. Taste and season accordingly; it should be a sweet and sour taste. Keep warm while frying fish. Discard bay leaves before serving.

Sauté sole in 1/8 inch canola oil in a skillet on medium-high until golden brown on both sides. Arrange fish in one layer on a large oval platter. While fish is still warm, pour sauce over, sprinkle with raisins, pine nuts and lots of chopped parsley. Refrigerate at least 2 hours before serving. Serve at room temperature.

Serves 4 to 6

1980   *Under Ernest Fleischmann's direction, famed architect Frank Gehry created fiberglass spheres to hang from the shell to reflect and distribute sound to the orchestra. They replaced the Sonotubes (manufactured concrete forms for concrete columns), which Gehry and acoustician Christopher Jaffe had devised in 1970.*

PANSANELLA SALAD

Cubes of sourdough or sun-dried tomato bread

Extra-virgin olive oil

2 cloves of garlic, pressed

4 anchovies, mashed

1/2 cup olive oil

Juice and zest of 1 lemon

10 tomatoes, skinned, seeded, diced

2 each red, yellow and green bell peppers, cleaned, diced

2 red onions, diced

2 cucumbers, skinned, seeded, diced

3 spring onions, diced, including green tops

Fry bread cubes in extra-virgin olive oil in a skillet over low heat to make crisp croutons. Place in sealable plastic bag.

Make a dressing of the garlic, anchovies, 1/2 cup olive oil and lemon juice with zest in a bowl. Place in container with tight-fitting lid. Mix vegetables together in a sealable plastic bag. Just before serving, strain dressing over vegetables in a bowl and add croutons. May be served cold or at room temperature.

Serves 10 to 12

1981 *Leonard Bernstein and Ernest Fleischmann founded the Los Angeles Philharmonic Institute, a world-class training institute for young instrumentalists and conductors. Bernstein and Daniel Lewis were artistic directors, and subsequently Michael Tilson Thomas and Lynn Harrell headed the Institute. A number of these young people have returned as acclaimed professionals, including conductors Yakov Kreizberg, Keith Lockhart, and David Alan Miller.*

SPINACH WITH PINE NUTS AND BALSAMIC GLAZE

This recipe, from internationally acclaimed baritone Rodney Gilfry, will make spinach haters into spinach lovers. Its rich flavors and beautifully intense green color make it welcome on any plate. It's also great cold—and it only takes about three minutes to prepare.

2 cloves crushed garlic

3 tablespoons extra-virgin olive oil

1/4 cup fresh pine nuts

1/4 teaspoon salt

2 to 4 bunches of fresh spinach leaves, washed and thoroughly dried (I don't recommend baby spinach; it cooks up too mushy)

2 tablespoons aged balsamic vinegar

1/4 cup (about) sour cream

Get ready! The preparation is extremely quick, so you'll need to have all the ingredients ready and within easy reach before turning the stove on! Be sure to turn your exhaust fan on high: the steam created by the vinegar is highly acidic and you DON'T want to BREATHE it!

Here goes…

Place garlic, oil, pine nuts and salt in a heavy gauge stockpot on high heat. Stir it a bit until the pine nuts start to turn brown. Leaving the heat on high, add the spinach leaves all at once and stir (two double-handfuls for four people). When the spinach is half-wilted (about 30 seconds), add the vinegar and stir but keep your face out of that steam! The vinegar will mostly evaporate and make a wonderful glaze. Remove it all from the pot immediately so it stops cooking. Serve with a dollop of sour cream on each portion.

Serves 4

A Summer Picnic Menu from James Galway

"We often have it at home, in our garden with the hi-fi on real loud—like a Hollywood Bowl for two.

"Our menu is for four people. We insist on china plates and real glasses. Real silver (no plastic). Only paper serviettes are allowed. Our list includes serving spoons, corkscrew, can opener, and four place settings and salt and pepper."

Beluga Caviar on crackers
Cold Salmon Trout (page 151)
New Potato Salad in Yogurt and Dill Dressing (page 153)
Mixed leafy green salad with cherry tomatoes, herbs,
*   spring onions and toasted pine nuts*
Freshly baked Ciabatta bread
Fresh Strawberries (page 154)

★ ★ ★ ★ ★ ★ ★ ★ ★ ★ ★ ★ ★ ★ ★ ★ ★

COLD SALMON TROUT

"We live in a little village on the lake with many fishers who bring us beautiful fresh seaforelle (sea trout). We have enjoyed many a quiet evening in our garden with this recipe. We enjoy it so much we have taken it on tour and adapted it to many species of trout and salmon. Whether wild salmon or lake trout, it is still delicious as long as the fish is fresh. (Always look for clear eyes when choosing a fish.)"

1 whole salmon or trout, approximately 1.5 kilos (about 4 pounds)
Freshly milled salt and white pepper
1 to 2 lemons, sliced
Cucumber Dill Sauce (page 152)

Rinse the fish inside and out under cold running water. Wipe with damp kitchen paper. Then place it in the center of a large sheet of foil. Salt and pepper the cavity (which has been cleaned by your fishmonger) and add a few lemon slices. Wrap the foil over the salmon to make a loose but tightly sealed parcel. Place the foil-wrapped fish on a wire rack above the broil pan. Bake for 25 to 30 minutes in a preheated 200 to 220 degrees (depending on your oven) Celsius (400 to 450 degrees F.).

   Test after 25 minutes by opening the foil (be careful of the steam) and pulling on the back fin (in middle of back of fish). If it comes out easily your fish is cooked perfectly.

   You can cool in the foil or out. Fillet into large pieces—transport filleted. Serve with lemon or our Cucumber Dill Sauce.

Serves 6 to 8

1984   *The Hollywood Bowl Museum was established by Ernest Fleischmann and County Supervisor Edmund D. Edelman to showcase the rich history of the Hollywood Bowl.*

CUCUMBER DILL SAUCE

1/2 cup natural yogurt

Dash tarragon wine vinegar

Juice of 1/2 lemon

2 tablespoons chopped fresh dillweed

Freshly milled salt and pepper

1/2 English cucumber with skin, or 1 whole garden cucumber without skin

Mix all ingredients in a small bowl except cucumber. Roughly chop cucumber; peel if necessary. Add cucumber to already mixed sauce. Season to taste. Refrigerate and transport in small Tupperware® container.

Serves 6 to 8

1985 *After making a highly successful American debut with the Los Angeles Philharmonic in 1984, Esa-Pekka Salonen appeared at the Bowl. Since then, his annual appearances are always welcomed by enthusiastic capacity audiences. A champion of today's music, Salonen sometimes includes his own compositions in the Philharmonic's programs.*

NEW POTATO SALAD IN YOGURT AND DILL DRESSING

2 pounds of small new potatoes (red or white)

Salt (ideally rock salt)

1 sprig of fresh mint (optional)

Freshly ground pepper

1/2 to 1 cup plain yogurt

1/4 to 1/2 cup finely chopped fresh dillweed

Rinse potatoes; scrub well (but carefully as the skins are light and full of nutrients) under cold water. Bring a large saucepan of water to a boil adding a bit of salt and if you like a sprig of mint. Place the largest potato on the base of the pan, with smaller ones on top. (Water should cover not more than three-quarters of the way up.) Cover tightly and boil for approximately 20 minutes—test with a skewer—potatoes should be of a floury texture (according to Irish tradition).

   Pour water out leaving potatoes in pan and place a tea towel over the pan and cover with lid. Place for a minute or two on the warm burner (which should be turned off). This will steam the extra moisture out of the potatoes (another Irish tip).

   Drain the potatoes in a colander and place in a metal bowl to cool. Halve them, salt and pepper them and add already combined dillweed and yogurt dressing while they're still hot. Mix thoroughly. Taste to check seasoning and keep salad in a cool place until needed. To transport, place in a tightly covered plastic bowl and lid (American Tupperware® is perfect).

Serves 8 to 10

FRESH STRAWBERRIES

"This is another Italian recipe we learned how to make while on vacation in Italy. It is light, refreshing and perfect for a concert. A beautiful end for a perfect evening."

500 grams (1 pound) strawberries, rinsed, halved
1 cup freshly squeezed orange juice
3 tablespoons freshly chopped mint
Freshly chopped mint

Prepare 1 hour before leaving or the morning of. Clean the strawberries. (We always looked for medium to small, very red ones—they are normally tastier.)

Squeeze juice from fresh oranges and pour over the strawberries. Add 3 tablespoons freshly chopped mint (not too finely chopped). Refrigerate. Keep cold. Garnish with additional chopped mint.

Serves 4 to 6

1990 *The Mariachi Festival was launched. It remains one of the pillars of preseason events. Two nights of this exciting music bring capacity audiences, who listen to world-famous exponents of mariachi.*

Pianist Steven Hough Menu

This menu is designed for a pre- or post-concert picnic, and aims to allow for equal taste-bud and ear-drum stimulation—minimizing the use of eating utensils and thus maximizing the ability to watch the concert with full concentration.

A large, soft, yet crusty white loaf

A substantial brick of Parmesan cheese

A container of pâté for each person (see recipe below)

A fine California Cabernet

Three large airtight containers, with inch-square chunks of pineapple, nectarine, and Cranshaw melon. These can be marinated in an alcoholic drink if desired, or instead, just a shower of fresh lemon juice.

A giant-size slab of bittersweet chocolate (72% cocoa) broken into shards of different sizes.

An ample flask of decaffeinated French-roast coffee.

Pâté (below)

★ ★ ★ ★ ★ ★ ★ ★ ★ ★ ★ ★ ★ ★ ★ ★ ★ ★ ★ ★

Pate

Take two-thirds full-flavor black olives, one-third sun-dried tomatoes, and some cloves of fresh garlic—amount depending on quantity of pâté to be prepared. Chop the garlic very finely, and the olives and tomatoes coarsely. Leave to soak overnight in some extra-virgin olive oil. Drain well and serve as a "scoop" (rather than "dip") with bread.

PEGGY LEE'S PICNIC SALAD EXTRAVAGANZA MENU

Miss Lee, a favorite of Hollywood Bowl-goers, last appeared in concert there in 1995. She died in January 2002.

Curried Chicken Salad (page 157)

Smoked Turkey Salad (page 158)

Three-Pepper Salad (page 159)

Wild Rice Salad Page (page 160)

Cold Sesame Noodles (page 161)

Melon, Shrimp and Avocado Salad (page 162)

★ ★ ★ ★ ★ ★ ★ ★ ★ ★ ★ ★ ★ ★ ★ ★ ★ ★ ★

1991 *The Hollywood Bowl Orchestra began its tenure under John Mauceri, a protégé of Leonard Bernstein. A leader in the preservation of two of America's great art forms, the American musical and film music, Mauceri and the Hollywood Bowl Orchestra spotlight many neglected masterpieces through their concerts and recordings.*

CURRIED CHICKEN SALAD

Salad

4 pounds boneless skinless chicken breasts

2 onions, cut into halves

1 parsnip, cut into quarters

2 bay leaves

10 sprigs of parsley

$1/2$ teaspoon salt

$1/4$ teaspoon freshly ground pepper

2 whole cloves

2 (8-ounce) cans sliced water chestnuts, drained

$3/4$ cup diagonally sliced scallions

Grated zest of 3 limes

Creamy Mango Dressing

$1^1/2$ cups mayonnaise

$1^1/2$ cups mango chutney, finely chopped

$1/3$ cup curry powder, or to taste

3 tablespoons soy sauce

For the salad, combine the chicken and onions with enough cold water to cover in a large saucepan. Bring to a boil. Add the parsnip, bay leaves, parsley, salt, pepper and cloves. Reduce the heat.

Simmer for 10 to 12 minutes or until the chicken is cooked through. Transfer the chicken to a colander using a slotted spoon and discarding the broth. Cool slightly. Cut the chicken into $1/2$- to $3/4$-inch pieces and place in a bowl. Stir in the water chestnuts, scallions and lime zest.

For the dressing, combine the mayonnaise, chutney, curry powder and soy sauce in a bowl and mix well. Add the dressing to the chicken mixture and mix well. Chill, covered, until serving time.

Serves 10 to 12

SMOKED TURKEY SALAD

Salad

2 3/4 pounds fresh smoked turkey breast

2 medium onions, minced

1 red bell pepper, cut into 1/2-inch pieces

1 cup fresh peas or frozen uncooked peas

3/4 cup finely chopped fresh parsley

Dressing

1 cup mayonnaise

1 tablespoon white wine vinegar

1 1/2 teaspoons freshly ground pepper

1 teaspoon salt

This recipe should be made at least 8 hours before serving to allow the flavors to blend.

For the salad, remove the skin and fat from the turkey and discard. Cut the turkey into 1/2- to 3/4-inch chunks and place in a salad bowl. Add the bell pepper, peas and parsley and mix well.

For the dressing, combine the mayonnaise, vinegar, pepper and salt in a bowl and mix well. Add the dressing to the turkey mixture and toss to coat. Chill, covered, until serving time.

Serves 6 to 8

1994　*Van Cliburn appeared with the Moscow Philharmonic during World Cup Week and was scheduled to play two concerts, as he had done 35 years earlier. He became indisposed during the course of the evening and replaced the Rachmaninoff Third Concerto with a series of solo encores.*

THREE-PEPPER SALAD

4 red bell peppers
4 green bell peppers
4 yellow bell peppers
2/3 cup olive oil

2 teaspoons salt
Dijon Vinaigrette (below)
3 tablespoons chopped fresh chives

Cut the bell peppers lengthwise into quarters, discarding the seeds and membranes. Coat the bell peppers with some of the olive oil. Arrange the bell peppers in a single layer in a large shallow baking dish. Drizzle with the remaining olive oil and sprinkle with the salt

Roast at 425 degrees for 20 minutes. Let stand until room temperature. Arrange the bell peppers overlapping on a serving platter. Drizzle with the Dijon Vinaigrette and sprinkle with the chives. Chill, covered, in the refrigerator for several hours. Bring to room temperature before serving.

Serves 10 to 12

DIJON VINAIGRETTE

3/4 cup olive oil
1/4 cup red wine vinegar
4 teaspoons Dijon mustard
1 teaspoon sugar

1/4 teaspoon Tabasco sauce
1 teaspoon minced garlic
1 teaspoon salt

Combine the olive oil, vinegar, Dijon mustard, sugar and Tabasco sauce in a jar with a tight-fitting lid. Mash the garlic and salt in a bowl until of a pasty consistency. Add the garlic mixture to the olive oil mixture and seal tightly. Shake to mix.

Makes 1 cup

WILD RICE SALAD

2 quarts water

8 ounces wild rice

1/2 teaspoon salt

1/2 cup hazelnuts, toasted, skinned, cut into halves

1/3 cup red wine vinegar

1/4 cup olive oil

3 scallions, chopped

1 orange

1 cup seedless red grape halves

1 teaspoon salt

1 teaspoon freshly ground pepper

Combine the water, wild rice and 1/2 teaspoon salt in a saucepan. Bring to a boil; reduce the heat. Simmer for 25 minutes or until the rice is al dente; drain. Spoon the rice into a salad bowl.

Add the hazelnuts, vinegar, olive oil and scallions to the rice and mix well. Zest the orange and add the zest to the rice mixture. Discard the white pith of the orange and chop the pulp. Add the chopped orange pulp to the rice mixture and mix well. Stir in the grapes, 1 teaspoon salt and pepper.

Let stand at room temperature for 30 minutes to allow the flavors to marry. Chill, covered, in the refrigerator for several hours. Bring to room temperature before serving.

Serves 4 to 6

1999   *The Hollywood Bowl launched a new Sunday evening series of World Music concerts, and the Clayton-Hamilton Jazz Orchestra was featured as the Bowl's resident jazz orchestra on Wednesdays throughout the season.*

COLD SESAME NOODLES

1 pound spaghettini
Salt to taste
2 tablespoons vegetable oil
Oriental Dressing (below)
1 green bell pepper, chopped
1 red bell pepper, chopped
1 small zucchini, cut lengthwise into
   halves, sliced

1 small yellow squash, cut lengthwise
   into halves, sliced
1 cup sliced water chestnuts
4 ounces snow peas, blanched,
   diagonally sliced
6 scallions, chopped
1/4 cup minced gingerroot

Break the pasta into halves or thirds. Combine the pasta and salt with enough water to cover in a saucepan. Bring to a boil. Boil until al dente; drain. Transfer the pasta to a bowl. Toss the pasta with the oil.

    Pour the Oriental Dressing over the pasta and toss until coated. Add the bell peppers, zucchini, yellow squash, water chestnuts, snow peas, scallions and gingerroot and mix well. Chill, covered, in the refrigerator for several hours. Bring to room temperature before serving.

Serves 8 to 10

ORIENTAL DRESSING

1/4 cup garlic cloves
1/2 cup peanut oil
1/2 cup tahini
1/2 cup strong tea
1/2 cup soy sauce

1/4 cup sugar
2 teaspoons freshly ground
   black pepper
1/8 teaspoon cayenne pepper

Pulse the garlic in a food processor until finely chopped. Add the peanut oil, tahini and tea. Pulse to blend. Add the soy sauce, sugar, black pepper and cayenne pepper. Pulse until blended and of a dressing consistency.

Makes 2 cups

MELON, SHRIMP AND AVOCADO SALAD

Juice of 1^1/2 lemons
2^1/2 avocados, cut into bite-size pieces
1^1/2 pounds peeled cooked shrimp
1^1/2 cantaloupes, cut into bite-size pieces
^{1}/2 honeydew melon, cut into bite-size pieces
^{1}/2 to ^{3}/4 cup finely chopped red onion
Curry Dressing (below)
Sprigs of fresh mint

Drizzle the lemon juice over the avocados in a salad bowl. Add the shrimp, cantaloupes, honeydew melon and red onion and gently mix.

Pour the Curry Dressing over the shrimp mixture and toss to coat. Chill, covered, until serving time. Garnish with sprigs of fresh mint just before serving.

Serves 6 to 8

CURRY DRESSING

^{1}/2 cup olive oil
2 tablespoons red wine vinegar
2 tablespoons heavy cream
1 garlic clove, minced
1 tablespoon curry powder
1 egg yolk, lightly beaten

Combine the olive oil, vinegar, heavy cream, garlic, curry powder and egg yolk in a jar with a tight-fitting lid and seal tightly. Shake to mix.

To avoid raw eggs that may carry salmonella, we suggest using an equivalent amount of pasteurized egg substitute.

Makes 1 cup

CHRISTOPHER HOGWOOD'S MENU

"For a grand Picnic in the authentic Manner!"

Grand Sallet (below)
French Bread (page 164)
Baked or Broiled Salmon (page 166)
Summer Pudding (page 167)

★ ★

A GRAND SALLET [SALAD]

Grand Sallet (Robert May, The Accomplisht Cook: Or, The Art and Mystery of Cookery, 1660)

All sort of good herbs, the little leaves of red sage; the smallest leaves of sorrel and the leaves of parseley picked very small, the youngest and smallest leaves of spinage, some leaves of burnet, the smallest leaves of lettice, white endive and charvel all finely pickt and washed and well drained from the water; then dish it in a clean scoured dish, and about the centre capers, currants, olives, lemons carved and sliced, boiled beetroots carved and sliced and dished round with good oyl and vinegar.

This recipe needs little translation. It is excellent when executed literally, but for that you need a kitchen garden—not many supermarkets stock red sage, sorrel, salad burnet (*Sanguisorba minor*) or chervil. But if the first phrase is interpreted as encapsulating the essence of May's intention, then a varied selection of greens of differing flavours can be combined to produce a delectable, even grand, salad. In the center a predominance of beet (freshly boiled, not pickled) and olives (salty Greek dry ones) seems to appeal to twenty-first century palates, with only a middling amount of capers and very few currants and peeled lemon cut small. Olive oil and wine vinegar can be sprinkled directly onto the greens or can first be mixed into a vinaigrette separately and then poured round.

FRENCH BREAD

To make French bread the best way (Robert May, The Accomplisht Cook: Or, The Art and Mystery of Cookery, 1660)

Take a gallon (7 lb.) of fine flour, and a pint of good new ale barm or yeast, and put it to the flour, with the whites of six new laid eggs well beaten in a dish, and mixt with the barm in the middle of the flour, also three spoonfuls of fine salt: then warm some milk and fair water, and put to it, and make it up pretty stiff, being well wrought and worked up, cover it in a bowl or tray with a warm cloth till your oven be hot; then make it up either in rouls, or fashion it in little wooden dishes and bake it, being baked in a quick oven, chip it hot.

1 lb. 1 oz. of flour (preferably 85% wheat, but if not available then 12 oz. unbleached
   and 5 oz. wholewheat)
$^1/2$ oz. fresh yeast
6 oz. warm water
4 oz. warm milk
2 tsp. salt
1 egg white

Place flour in a large bowl. Dissolve yeast in 2 tbsp. of the warm milk and water mixture; make well in center of flour, pour in yeast mixture and salt and cover with flour. (Dry yeast can be used; follow instructions on packet.) Add the egg white, beaten in a small bowl until it is just beginning to froth. Pour in the remaining milk and water. Mix well and then knead, either in the bowl or on a floured board, for 10 minutes. Put the bowl into a large plastic bag and leave to rise at room temperature until doubled in size, about 1 hour.

Break down the dough, divide it into two equal portions and shape each into a long roll by flattening it into a rectangle and then rolling it up like a jelly roll. Put them on a greased baking tray. Cover with a sheet of polythene or a light cloth and leave them to recover volume, about 30 minutes. Meanwhile preheat the oven to 450°F.

When risen, place in center of hot oven. After 15 minutes turn oven down to 400°F and bake for another 15 minutes. If you intend to follow May's instructions exactly and "chip it hot," the crust must be quite hard.

I don't recommend chipping for any but those with a strong historical curiosity and no hang-ups about tidiness—crust chippings will rain down everywhere. If you still want to proceed, while the loaf is hot, take a heavy sharp knife, and holding it at a slight angle, hit the crust repeatedly with the sharp blade. Gradually the chips of crust begin to fly off and after about ten minutes the whole surface will "look spungy and of a fine yellow" (Hannah Glasse, 1746). According to Paul Jacques Malouin (Description des arte of motiers, Paris, 1767, in Barbara Ketcham Wheaton, *Savouring the Past*, 193), the chippings were sold 'to the poor and country people' to put in their soup. And lest you feel tempted to take a grater to the rolls instead of chipping them, Mrs. Glasse (1746) warns: "rasping takes off all the fine colour, and makes it look too smooth."

2001 *Hollywood High School seniors still use the Bowl for their commencement exercises, thanks to a long-ago promise given at the onset of Symphonies Under the Stars in 1922. Students at that time mounted a highly professional production of Shakespeare's* Twelfth Night, *committing the ticket sales proceeds in advance toward the purchase of a theatrical switchboard and footlights, which they used for the production and then donated to the Bowl.*

BAKED OR BOILED SALMON

To dress a salmon au court-bouillon (Patrick Lamb, Royal Cookery, 1710)

After having drawn and cleaned your salmon, score the sides of it pretty deep, that it may take the relish of your court-bouillon the better; lay it on a napkin and season it with salt, pepper, cloves, nutmeg, onions, chives, parsly, sliced lemon, bay leaf and basil. Work up the quantity of about a pound of butter with a little flower and put it into the belly of the salmon, then wrap the salmon in the napkin, bind it about with a packthread and lay it in a fish kettle. Put to it a quantity sufficient to boil it in, of wine, water and vinegar and set it over a quick fire. When it is done enough, take it off and keep it simmering over a stove, till you are ready. Garnish with green parsly.

3 lb. whole salmon	1 handful fresh parsley, chopped
salt	1 handful fresh basil, chopped
pepper	1 lemon, sliced thinly
powdered cloves	6 bay leaves
$1/3$ nutmeg, grated	1 tbsp. white wine vinegar
1 medium onion, chopped	1 tbsp. white wine
2 tbsp. fresh chives, chopped	1 oz. parsley sprigs

If you wish to be authentically eighteenth century, then follow Patrick Lamb's instructions above. Otherwise, tear off a piece of foil large enough to wrap your salmon loosely (use a double thickness for greater strength). Paint the foil with olive oil. Score the sides of the salmon deeply. Season well inside and out with salt and pepper. Sprinkle sparingly with cloves and nutmeg. Spread half the onion, herbs, lemon slices and bay leaves in the center of the foil and place the salmon on top. Put the remainder of the onion, herbs, lemon and bay leaves on top. Sprinkle with the wine vinegar and wine and fold the edges of the foil tightly together to make a sealed parcel. Bake at 350 degrees for 40 to 50 minutes. Remove from oven, leave to cool in the foil and then chill in the refrigerator. When chilled, open foil, scrape off herbs and remove skin. Cut salmon into serving portions and garnish liberally with parsley sprigs. Lemon slices or wedges are a good additional garnish.

Serves 4

166

SUMMER PUDDING

Everyone knows, or thinks they know, that summer pudding is as old and traditional an English dessert as syllabub or fool. My mother calls it Dr. Johnson's pudding. But none of my seventeenth or eighteenth century cookery books give a recipe for anything of the kind. 'Raspberry and Currant Pudding' in the 1909 edition of Mrs. Beeton consists of bread layered with bottled fruit, but the recipe is missing from the first edition of 1859. Despite its lack of historical documentation, my favorite recipe is:

1 loaf of homemade thinly sliced white bread (country French or Italian bread might have a
   good enough flavor and texture to substitute, a supermarket packaged loaf does not)
1 lb fresh raspberries
4 oz red currants
1 to 1 1/2 cups sugar
8 oz whipped cream

Cut crust from slices of bread and line a 1-quart bowl with a single layer of bread. Trim the slices so they fit tightly together without gaps.

Beat the raspberries, red currants and sugar together in a bowl with a wooden spoon. In under a minute the fruit will begin to break down and release its juices. There is no need to cook it. Taste and add more sugar if desired.

Place half the fruit mixture into the bread-lined bowl. Cover it with a layer of bread cut to fit. Pour in the rest of the fruit mixture and cover with a layer of bread cut to fit tightly. Place a plate that will just fit inside the rim of the bowl on top and a weight on top of the plate (a can of tomatoes works well). Leave in the refrigerator for several hours to allow the fruit juices to permeate the bread.

Either package individual portions in separate containers or transport in the bowl and take whipped cream in a separate container. To serve, turn out onto a plate, cut into portions and spoon on whipped cream.

Serves 4

PICNIC EQUIPMENT

The best of all picnicking worlds includes a beautiful, fully equipped picnic basket, with matched sets of plates, bowls, utensils, crystal, and linens. Sometimes that is possible, but, when it isn't, ingenuity must take over. Any large basket with a strong handle can be used, lined with a colorful towel and filled with plastic and paper utensils and plates. Or, go shopping at yard sales and thrift stores for your picnic supplies—things may not match but will add charm to any picnic atmosphere. Tote bags make very good picnic "baskets" and are easy to carry. Insulated ice chests come in all sizes (some with wheels), and insulated bags are lighter weight for easier handling.

And then there are those times when the "picnic basket" is a large brown paper bag straight from the grocery store with paper plates and plastic utensils!

Regardless of the means of transportation, a basic list of suggested equipment is essential so that you can relax and enjoy the occasion with your friends, family, or guests.

Tablecloth and napkins

Forks, knives, and spoons

Dinner plates

Small plates for hors d'oeuvre, salads, or desserts

Coffee cups

Soup bowls

Wine glasses

Corkscrew or can and bottle openers

Serving spoons and utensils

Bread knife and cutting board

Small sharp knife

Salt and pepper

Small flashlight

Plastic bags for cleanup

Paper towels

Wash 'n dries for both before and after eating

GENERAL HINTS

Think about packing and transporting your food while you plan your menu. Can it be put into a container easily? Will it look attractive after being wrapped, carried, and perhaps jostled?

The perfect picnic food is one that can be eaten out of hand. Sandwiches, barbecued ribs, dips and crackers, deviled eggs, muffins, rolls, and cookies are all in the hand-to-mouth category. Foods that require only a fork or spoon to eat (no cutting) include thick soups; picnic salads, such as potato, chicken, fruit, and macaroni; entrée and dessert pies; and cakes.

Slice and reassemble meats, pies, cakes, etc., at home for ease in serving at the picnic site. Foods cooked in a springform pan can be cut at home, removing the ring and then replacing it again for transport.

Pack your picnic carrier, as much as possible, in the sequence in which you will use it. Of course, heavy things should be packed at the bottom, not the top.

Fill empty spaces in your basket, bag, or chest with crumpled newspaper to keep foods from sliding and to assist with temperature control.

Tape down any screw-top or other lidded containers to prevent leaks and to keep them from popping open.

Carry chilled salad greens in a plastic bag and the dressing in a separate container. If the bag isn't too full, the salad can be "tossed" in the bag. Just pour the dressing over the greens, reseal the bag, leaving plenty of air space, and shake gently.

Large napkins are almost essential when eating outdoors, where finger food menus and plates balanced on laps are frequently the norm. Small tea towels also can make excellent napkins, or use them for lap cloths when sitting on the ground.

KEEPING COLD FOOD COLD...

It is most important to thoroughly chill food that should be served cold before packing it and transporting it to the picnic area. Do not rely on the ice that you pack things in to lower the temperature. Even the food that is to be served at room temperature, especially meats, should be chilled before you leave home.

To keep cold foods cold longer, use two sets of disposable foil pans. Fill one partially with water and freeze; stack the other pan inside the one with the ice and put your food in it.

When you are outdoors, keep the food and cooler out of direct sunlight. And remember, before returning home, discard any perishables that have been at room temperature for several hours.

Dry ice is the only portable refrigerant that will keep food frozen. It should be wrapped in newspapers and placed on top of frozen foods. Never handle dry ice with bare hands.

Generally, baked goods should be thoroughly cooled before being sealed and packed.

Prechill thermos containers with ice water.

To transport cold foods, use an insulated chest or bags. Use a plastic bag of ice cubes, frozen containers of refrigerant gel, homemade ice blocks sealed in plastic bags, or dry ice wrapped in layers of newspaper. Place these on top of anything to be kept cold, as cold air travels downward.

...AND HOT FOOD HOT

Time the food preparation so that anything that should be served hot goes directly from the stove or oven to the picnic.

A thoroughly cooked casserole will usually stay hot if you insulate it with foil, followed by several layers of newspaper and a towel. This also makes hot dishes easier to carry.

Look for insulated zipper bags at specialty stores or in catalogues. They come in different sizes, but the one most frequently found fits a 9x13-inch baking pan.

Heat a flat brick or piece of slate in the oven while baking your picnic fare. Wrap it in a single sheet of newspaper and then place it under the hot food container so that it can be incorporated into the foil and newspaper insulating wrap.

Preheat thermos containers with boiling water before filling with hot liquids.

INDEX

INDEX

The Hollywood Bowl Cookbook: Picnics Under the Stars

Los Angeles Philharmonic Affiliates
P.O. Box 1951
Hollywood, California 90078

_____
Name

_____
Street Address

_____
City   State   Zip

_____
Telephone

YOUR ORDER	QUANTITY	TOTAL
The Hollywood Bowl Cookbook at $19.95 per book		$
California residents add sales tax at $2.14 per book		$
Postage and handling at $6.00 per book		$
	TOTAL	$

Method of Payment: [   ] MasterCard   [   ] VISA

                      [   ] Check payable to Los Angeles Philharmonic Affiliates

_____
Account Number   Expiration Date

_____
Signature

Proceeds from the sale of *The Hollywood Bowl Cookbook: Picnics Under the Stars*
will benefit the Los Angeles Philharmonic.

Also available at the Hollywood Bowl Gift Shop.

Photocopies will be accepted.